THE STATE OF US

www.penguin.co.uk

THE STATE OF US

*The good news and the bad news
about our society*

JON SNOW

bantam

TRANSWORLD PUBLISHERS
Penguin Random House, One Embassy Gardens,
8 Viaduct Gardens, London SW11 7BW
www.penguin.co.uk

Transworld is part of the Penguin Random House group of companies
whose addresses can be found at global.penguinrandomhouse.com

Penguin
Random House
UK

First published in Great Britain in 2023 by Bantam
an imprint of Transworld Publishers

A CIP catalogue record for this book
is available from the British Library.

ISBNs 9781787635708 (cased)
9781787637467 (tpb)

Typeset in 14/17pt Granjon LT Std by Jouve (UK), Milton Keynes
Printed and bound in Great Britain by Clays Ltd, Elcograf S.p.A.

The authorized representative in the EEA is Penguin Random House Ireland,
Morrison Chambers, 32 Nassau Street, Dublin D02 YH68.

Penguin Random House is committed to a sustainable future
for our business, our readers and our planet. This book is made
from Forest Stewardship Council® certified paper.

For Precious and Tafara

CONTENTS

PREFACE

I WRITE THIS AS AUTUMN dawns in our state. The newspapers are littered with bitter forecasts of a scale of poverty few people living in Britain today have ever known. So bad is the crisis that former UN rapporteur Philip Alston accused Britain's Department for Work and Pensions of creating a 'digital and sanitised version' of the nineteenth-century workhouse. 'Lives will be lost' states the *Guardian* in its front-page headline, adding that 'typical gas and electricity bills [are] to rise 80% to £3,549 a year'. The Joseph Rowntree Foundation analysts say that the poorest single adults could see finances 'wiped out' by 'stratospheric' energy bills representing 120 per cent of their incomes after housing costs, leaving many destitute. The cynical tend to react by saying that the ruling Conservatives don't bank on many votes from the poor anyway.

This is set against a UN report written by Mr Alston in 2019 which stated that 'the social safety net that once protected the most vulnerable has been replaced with a harsh and uncaring ethos'. The Australian-born Alston, seventy-two, a human rights lawyer and professor at New York University's School of Law, believes the UK has twice been a 'social laboratory' regarding welfare: first in the aftermath of the Second World War, when the Beveridge Report outlined a blueprint for the introduction of a welfare state, and second when the Conservatives came to power in 2010. Indeed, in the first week of her brief tenure as prime minister, Liz Truss stated that she believed it was wrong 'to look at everything through the lens of redistribution'.

Amber Rudd, the former work and pensions secretary at the time Alston's report came out, said she was 'disappointed' by the 'extraordinarily political nature of the language' it contained, and threatened to complain to the UN. Alston says there has been no such complaint made to the UN. In my lifetime as a reporter, I have never known such senior figures warn of so unparalleled a moment of threatened deprivation in a founder member state of the UN itself. Alston describes what he regards as 'the extremely objective and high-quality analyses of charities in this field'. He continues, 'If employment is getting better, but at the same time food banks are having unprecedented levels of demand, that employment ain't enough? But they don't want to get into that debate.'

Despite the introduction of the welfare state in 1945, poverty in our society has if anything grown in my lifetime. I cannot recall seeing such dire threats in the headlines on anything like this scale. And given the high authority from which these warnings emerge, we have to take them very seriously. Indeed, by the time you are reading this, some of the worst may already be upon us. There is no doubt that, in common with countries all over the world, Britain faces a time of monumental challenge, from inflation and global supply chain issues to the worsening climate crisis. But that is also a signal for the world to come together, in a way that only the threats from the outbreak of war have ever occasioned in the past. It may seem odd to say so, but Covid-19 may have provided a helpful overture in uniting nations to combat an international threat. We will have to work collaboratively as never before in peacetime, and it will take leadership of which we have been in short supply for far too long. We simply cannot assume that the projections being made will turn out in some way to be mere exaggerations. We have to be fully prepared.

One of the beauties of British society is the volunteer ethic. Many people already dedicate themselves to improving the lives of others. The time may be fast approaching when we will each have to decide how much more we can contribute individually – not just financially, but spiritually and physically. We have to look after those who are going to need our assistance most, as many Britons did so generously for the tens of thousands of Ukrainians who have had to flee their homes. It is one thing to give cash; it's another to spot and respond to someone in our neighbourhood who desperately needs our help.

The cynic, who to some extent resides in all of us, may be tempted to say that somebody has got all this wrong; that it can't be as bad as all this; but in my experience what we are being told by too many sources is that this crisis is real, and we will have to change our ways.

PART ONE

SOCIETY

CHAPTER I

WAKE-UP CALL

WHEN I ARRIVED AT THE Channel 4 News studios, I heard that there'd been a fire in a building in the Borough of Kensington and Chelsea the night before. At first, I don't think anybody had a sense of the enormity of what was going on. Some colleagues brushed it off: 'Well, that's a London story, leave it to ITV.' But, very quickly, the information we were receiving started to sound very serious indeed. We began to get a sense that this was not just a little fire, one that would pass by without much incident – an awful lot of people were going to be affected by what was, we realized, an inferno. As pictures, tweets, messages and calls started to filter their way to the newsroom, we became aware that the fire had occurred in a tower block. It was an extremely tall building, and potentially hundreds of people were trapped inside. With horror, I saw that all the ingredients for an absolute disaster were in place.

I leapt on my bike, by far the quickest way to travel across town, and cycled over. The smoke cloud was a grievous horror, billowing up into the sky. It was visible from almost anywhere in London. I certainly didn't need a map to find Grenfell – I just headed towards the black column snaking up into the sky that rose in front of me as I left the back end of Paddington Station. Rounding the corner by the canals, I was struck by a feeling of two parallel existences. It was a glorious, sunny morning. People were in the parks, sat on tables in front of cafés, ties loosened, shirtsleeves rolled up. The carefree lives I was passing seemed a perverse foreshadowing of what I would find, just minutes away, in the Borough of Kensington and Chelsea.

I was naïve enough to imagine that Grenfell Tower would transpire to be a luxury high-rise, housing rich tenants. Not a bit of it – this was one of several council blocks housing families of working people. It's an easy mistake to make. When we say Kensington and Chelsea, we tend to conjure images of wealth and glitz; we over-look the fact that the borough is not just home to the upper-middle classes and has its share of working-class people who provide support for the whole community. And yet, in that moment, it was they who were crying out for support and rescue – neither of which, I might add, was very evident.

Despite my assumption about Grenfell Tower, I was not completely in the dark about the make-up of the bor-ough more generally. As I cycled towards the column of smoke rising into the sky, my thoughts turned to an event which I had attended just a few weeks previously. On 20 April 2017, just fifty days before the fire, I had been invited to judge, alongside Bill Gates, the co-founder of

Microsoft, a debating competition in London. It was the final of a countrywide championship organized by the charity Debate Mate. This is an organization that does fantastic work in democratizing that skill so often associated with the elite – public speaking. I attended as a judge of the best floor speech. There was little difficulty in deciding the winner. It was Firdaws Hashim, a remarkably poised twelve-year-old from West London. She was supremely confident and used language beautifully. Bill Gates grasped her hand when he gave her the award – like me, like everybody who witnessed her performance, he was absolutely blown away by the quality of her writing and her remarkable ability to present it with assurance and composure. Through her eloquence Firdaws demanded to be seen. She attended Kensington Aldridge Academy, whose buildings stood in the shadow of Grenfell. Firdaws seemed to represent that class that had too long been forgotten in Kensington and Chelsea. She did not come from a rich background; her parents weren't bankers or columnists or executives – rather, her father had that most iconic job of the working Londoner: he was a black-cab driver.

Pulling up on my bicycle, Grenfell Tower was very scarred and very red. It was burnt, yet it was still burning. The fire wasn't over by any means; the building continued to smoulder. There was something nightmarish and unnatural about its progress. One expects a fire to climb up a building, but this one was going down. The floors were catching one after the other, and the fire chased down from the top towards the ground. By the time I arrived the emergency services, and most particularly the fire brigade, were there in full force. They were accompanied by a helicopter which hovered and sprayed water from above. Attempts at rescue were under way. It was clear to me that the fire brigade were doing the best they possibly could, working desperately to try to enter the building and pull the victims out. But it was also clear that very few people could escape the floors affected, particularly those towards the top of Grenfell's twenty-four storeys.

With horror, I realized that I was watching a tragedy unfold in real time – a terrifying scene of death and despair. More than that, the inequality of the area stood out as starkly as the smoking building did against the summer sky. Quite literally one street away from Grenfell Tower there are picture-perfect Victorian crescents, the houses painted in pastel tones, so desirable that holiday-makers from around the world stand in front of them and take selfies. There are restaurants selling the finest cuisine, where a single 'small plate' costs more than a family in the Grenfell Tower had to spend on their weekly groceries. Here we were in the richest borough in Britain, and somehow matters had coalesced to produce the most appalling suffering amongst its poorest inhabitants. How, I wanted to know, could this possibly have happened?

We devoted the rest of the day to finding out. Who could we talk to, live on the programme, to give us a sense of the significance of what had happened? We interviewed many local people and the consistency of what they told us began a profound change in my outlook. As we sought to make sense of the emergency during those hours before we were transmitted at seven o'clock in the evening, it became very clear to me that this was an archetypal story of inequality. Over and over again we heard the same thing – people were ignored because they were poor, and poor because they were ignored. As Eddie Daffarn, a social worker who lived at Grenfell and whose blogging had warned of a potential fire catastrophe, put it: 'The reality is if you're on a housing estate it's indifference and neglect, two words that sum up everything about the way we were treated ... They weren't interested in providing housing services, keeping us safe, maintaining the estate. They were just interested in themselves.' The 'they' here refers to Kensington and Chelsea Council, but could just as easily have meant news organizations, politicians and financial institutions.[1]

As I said, my knee-jerk thought when I heard that a tower was on fire in Kensington was of a block of luxury flats. In truth, it is completely inconceivable that such a disaster would have been allowed to happen in a rich block: if the inhabitants are wealthy, they are very much better provisioned. The owners, who tend to be private companies rather than local authorities, know the scale of their duty to ensure that nothing ever goes wrong. I can't think of an instance in which well-off people have been burnt to death in a residential tower block. If

Grenfell had been occupied by bankers and people from the upper echelons of society, you sense that there would have been fire alarms, self-sealing doors and sprinklers. But it was ordinary people who lived at Grenfell, and many of them had come to this country from abroad. For them, there was no escape mechanism. Nobody with the power to do anything seemed to have dreamt of what would happen if the tower caught fire. That basic preparation hadn't happened. There were some very fundamental elements missing. Space in front of the building for emergency vehicles was compromised. Fire exits had been blocked. Tenants had not been briefed on what to do in case of emergency. As I talked to people in the immediate aftermath and interviewed some for the news, I was startled to find that there were several who thought it not surprising. Of course, there was a lot of distress because people had friends, neighbours and relatives in the tower; but the fire itself, and the difficulties associated with rescuing people, seemed to be of a piece with their wider experiences of life.

My growing feeling was that nobody in authority had ever thought about the needs of the kind of people who lived in Grenfell Tower. As a very crude and straightforward example, a number of people who lived there were migrants who weren't as aware as native-born Britons about which parts of the council you needed to talk to get things done: the infrastructure that existed to support them wasn't always accessible for them. Then, on a purely linguistic level, they may not have been able to understand the very specific language of a document about evacuation or safety. We know that tenants had not been given proper fire-safety instructions by the company who managed the building. There were no directions posted in the communal sections telling residents what to do in the event of a fire. There had been a recent newsletter which explained that residents should remain in their flats – advice that proved to be disastrous when followed – but, even if this advice had been accurate, a residents' newsletter is not many people's first port of call for safety instructions. Likewise, if they did not read English well, there's no guarantee that tenants could have understood the information even if they had wanted to and knew where to look. It should go without saying that information needs to be highly accessible – available in multiple languages, and comprehensible to a child – otherwise it's useless. But nobody who drafted those documents ever thought of that, and nobody who worked in the local political infrastructure seemed to have made an effort to change the system to meet the needs of the people it was supposed to serve. Of course, there are Acts of Parliament which dictate that a building like this must have certain kinds of resources. But that turned out to be worthless in the event – lip service had been paid to safety, exemplifying the old axiom regarding the letter of the law rather than its spirit. Ultimately, the inhabitants didn't have a channel via which to tell the authorities of their fears. There was no official record of people expressing anxiety about the danger of the building. The result, as we were on the ground reporting, was complete chaos. Nobody knew what to advise. Nobody had ever faced a similar situation. Nobody even knew the dangers posed by the building itself, by the fact that the cladding was flammable.

As the journalistic work wore on, the difficulties I faced ceased to be a question of filing a news report. I was now trying hard not to become completely overwhelmed by the experience. At moments – whilst I was walking around the estate, trying to talk to people and extract information – I was close to tears. I've been to disasters before, I've reported from war zones, but nothing, *nothing* jarred like this did. The collision between wealth and poverty defined the whole event. It was an extremely emotional experience.

I was down at the centre of the disaster for the best part of a week. After a couple of days, amongst the rows and rows of home-made posters, I spotted a photograph. In red writing at the top: Missing. On the right, a boy, in a yellow helmet, his gaze directly at us. On the left, a girl, perhaps ten, eleven. She too wears a yellow climbing helmet and, hauntingly, looks away from the camera to her right, her eyes focusing on something out of shot. *Missing since early morning 14/6/17.*

Unmistakably, it was Firdaws. The girl I had just weeks earlier, with Bill Gates at my side, judged as the best young public speaker in the country was, unbeknownst to me, a resident of Grenfell Tower. This brilliant girl lived with her family on the twenty-second floor. I knew precisely what the poster meant. I knew precisely what had happened.

And at this moment, I burst into tears.

The state of us

Many countries around the world are experiencing an existential upheaval. It is rare in history for so many nations in the developed world to suffer such a crisis at one and the same time: the belief that parliamentary structures are no longer fit for purpose; the doubts centred upon whether the democratic system is any longer capable of serving their needs; and above all, the disintegration of trust in political leadership.

Key amongst these issues is inequality. For all the progress humankind has made, for all the inventions, for all the discoveries and new technologies, Western societies are severely undermined by social inequality. Here in the UK, the richest 1 per cent of households earn around 150 times more than the poorest. Likewise, that top 1 per cent also own 13 per cent of our nation's wealth – meaning that inequality in wealth is greater than the already very great inequality of income. The richest 5 per cent of people in the UK own 950 times as much as the poorest 5 per cent.[2]

Is inequality inherently bad? Is it not to be expected that some people achieve at a higher level than others? Perhaps we shouldn't overburden ourselves with concern, just so long as that 1 per cent are, quite simply, the best of us. Perhaps. But they aren't. According to researchers at the London School of Economics, 'Social mobility – the ability of people to move up the social ladder – is getting harder; a child born in 1970 has much less chance of ending up as a top earner than a child born in 1958.'[3] For those born in the 1980s and 1990s, things are worse. In fact, on all these measures, as time goes by inequality seems to be increasing – both in terms of outcome and in terms of opportunity. For most of the twentieth century, inequality was flat or falling in the UK. Where have we gone wrong?

Grenfell remains an alarming wake-up call. In one drastic failure in one tower block, we see the essence of inequality horrifically exemplified. From the elevated Westway motorway route into London, to this day Grenfell stands shrouded in canvas to prevent us from seeing the fire-blackened façade and burnt-out concrete. The numbers and figures in the above paragraph are shocking, but I fear they do little to jolt us from our stupor. Surely, as we stare out from our cars south to Grenfell Tower before turning eastwards to the City of London – and the towers of the Shard, the Gherkin and 22 Bishopsgate – we must realize that something is wrong. Inequality is not undesirable simply because of its adverse impact on productivity and economic growth, and not even because of the political chaos that ensues from living in an unjust society. Inequality strikes us in our hearts, too: it's wrong. It's wrong that that no one in the council appeared to have worked out whether a child like

Firdaws, or even an adult like her father, would be able safely to escape their home if it caught fire. It's wrong that some of us don't have enough money to eat whilst others fly wagyu beef halfway across the planet for a couple of amusing mouthfuls. It is worth remembering that approximately 2.5 million people in the UK rely on a food bank.[4] It's wrong that there are talented young people up and down this country whose intelligence is wasted in exhausting, poorly paid manual labour when those without qualifications are given plum jobs in the media simply because of where they went to school. And I can include myself in that group, despite a lack of academic achievement.

I am not one of life's scholars. I have worked hard over the course of my career, and I'm proud of my accomplishments. But there are many other people with only six O-Levels and a C, a D and an E at A-Level who did not go on to read the news on television. Now I don't think my career is entirely due to my background. But it is abundantly clear to me that despite my ambition and drive, and despite a few unusual tools in my locker, I was born with an advantage over many others. I realize it's an absurd situation to talk about inequality when one is, in fact, a member of the elite. I'm fully aware of it. But nevertheless, I have been a journalist for over fifty years now and, having spent most of my life trying to explain to the nation what is going on, I find myself, at the end of my career, with an answer to the question and the freedom to be able to state it. Inequality is the story behind so many other stories. It is the key issue at the heart of everything that is going on today. This book, then, is an attempt to explain how I came to this conclusion.

What do I mean when I use these words? What is an elite? What is inequality? In Britain, both centre on class, which has been historically constructed and has proved a long-lasting element of Britishness. I wouldn't say that the issue of class and social division has altered in any significant way since I was born. There are moments when I thought things were changing, but then I made new discoveries. Largely, class is informed by education, by whether you and your parents were educated at a private school. The public-school system hasn't changed at all as far as I can tell. There are some girls in some of the boys' schools, but I don't think that has fundamentally altered our shared reality. There is still no question that in buying a private education, you're buying a better chance for your child. Otherwise, what would be the point? That being the case, class remains an inescapable fact of life in Britain.

Having said that, and to head off certain expected criticisms, I'm not a communist. I'm not looking for blind equality, or even equality of outcomes in general. Neither am I a pathological anti-private-education type. I believe simply in equality of opportunity. It's very difficult to bring about and, as I mentioned, we haven't gone an enormous way in doing so over the course of my life, and I've been knocking around for more than seventy years.

But we can, and we must, improve. We have to recognize what the consequences are if we don't. Consequences like Grenfell. If we are serious about ensuring that something like that terrible fire doesn't happen again, we have to start offsetting the differences between the privileged and everybody else.

The basic argument of this book is that across society, in various fields, there has been a process of elite capture that has disenfranchised the average person. Elite capture is the process by which public resources, which should benefit everybody, fail to do so because economically, politically and/or socially advantaged groups hijack that resource and make it serve their own, far narrower interest. This divorces person from person, community from community, individual from society, and society from institutions. To address this, I've split the book in two parts.

The first takes us through glaring examples of inequality in Britain and around the world. We shall investigate the old institutions that helped create an elite in the UK – the public schools, the Church, and the hereditary nature of some of our political institutions. We'll look at where we live, and see the role played by housing and property wealth in establishing the inequality that divides us, and what the lethal consequences can be. We'll investigate how this inequality plays out at the national level, focusing on Brexit – undoubtedly the hardest moment of my reporting career – before finally considering international inequality and its threat to peace. As I write this, Vladimir

Putin has taken his armies into a war with Ukraine that conveys no apparent benefit to the Russian people at large. It puts me in mind of 2003, when, despite much public opposition, Tony Blair took Britain to war in Iraq. Despite the difference in the two political systems, the result is the same. Is there a more brutal illustration of the elite's power over the common man than the executive sending young soldiers to die in ill-thought-out military campaigns?

The second section looks more specifically at the world that I've inhabited for the past fifty years: journalism and news media. I believe that journalism is, potentially, one of the best defences against inequality that we have. But it has the ability to drive inequalities too. Here, I'll take on a challenge mounted by elites against ordinary people in three ways and show how that has affected the news. In the first, it's how private interest groups can capture the news – online, in print, or broadcast – because they have a vested interest in making the information you see flatter them. In the second, we'll look at governments at home and abroad and their attempts to deaden the conversation so that the average person can't see what's really happening, deflecting criticism where and when it's due. A free press is a hallowed right that we have had to fight for, close to home and far away, and it's under threat. Finally, we'll look at how newsrooms themselves are beset by the inequalities of our society at large. This means that important issues of race, class and gender get missed – ultimately, if all journalists are white, upper- or middle-class and male (like me), they are going to have blind spots and miss stories.

Gazing up at the smoke still pouring from Grenfell Tower in the early hours, I felt the weight of the journalist's obligation to understand what had happened. The seeds for this book were sown then. When I reflected upon the power contradictions between those who had suffered and died in the blaze and those who administer the local authority, in whose hands this scandalous failure had occurred, I felt both disconnected and frustrated. I was on the wrong side of the terrible divide that exists in present-day society and in which we are all major players. We can accuse the political classes of their failures, and we do. But all of us – myself included – are guilty. This country is becoming stratified and divided. People like me have grown too far removed from those who lived their lives in Grenfell and who, across the country, still live in homes with combustible cladding, no sprinklers and without centralized fire alarms.

Amidst the demonstrations around Grenfell after the fire there were cries of 'Where were you, Snow? Why didn't you come here before?' It's a very fair question. Why didn't we? Why didn't we have contact? Why didn't we know what was going on? Why didn't we enable the residents of Grenfell Tower – and indeed the other hundreds of tower blocks like it around Britain – to find ways to talk to us and for us to expose their stories? We had missed it. What we thought was going on was not the whole story. And some of it we got wrong.

In the recent past, politicians, journalists, pundits, pollsters and other so-called experts have got it wrong repeatedly. The Brexit referendum – most in the media predicted the wrong outcome. Trump becoming president in America completely defied the expectations of yet more experts and media operatives. Did we predict the rise of neo-fascism in parts of Europe, or recognize it for what it was when it dawned? In Britain, Prime Minister Theresa May unnecessarily called a general election in 2017. It was predicted to give her a majority of sixty to seventy seats in Parliament. We got that wrong too. She was forced to do a deal with hard-line Ulster nationalists in Northern Ireland to stay in power. And it was this that we were discussing in the days before the fire. May's electoral failure was just a week earlier, and the principal issue of the day was Brexit. Given what we uncovered at Grenfell – a citizenry that felt ignored, and inequality running rampant – should we have been so seriously surprised to find that the vast majority of the most challenging places to live in Britain voted to kick the people in power in the teeth?[5]

That electoral failure by Theresa May, that Trump triumph, that Brexit shock result, that once-improbable Boris Johnson premiership – I believe their cause was uniform. I will set out my contention that widespread distress, kindled by inequality, played a devastating role in delivering unexpected votes that rocked electoral predictions across the Western world, leaving a trail of division in its wake.

Who am I?

I want to talk about how my experiences over what is now a reasonably long career have informed my point of view. That's because, before I'm anything else, I am a journalist. You may know me because I have read the Channel 4 News at 7 p.m. since the late 1980s. But over the course of my life I've reported from all kinds of places and uncovered all kinds of stories. I believe in the power of journalism to change the world. I believe, ultimately, that if journalists do their job properly, if they report the facts accurately, pursue the truth doggedly and tell the story impartially, the public can make up their own minds about what to do, either at the ballot box or in their every-day lives.

Whilst I am a member of the elite, life knocked me about a bit as a young man. Prior to my journalism career, I became entangled with what I saw as the burning injustice of the day – apartheid. It ended up costing me my degree. So I have the unusual combination of being from the elite but also being on the receiving end of its unforgiving judgement. There were other early experiences, too, that shaped who I am today. Two stand out, which I'll detail in later chapters: my time in Uganda working with Voluntary Service Overseas, and my life-long involvement with the homeless charity New

Horizon. Both were incredible. Both profoundly changed my outlook on life.

These early experiences made it a bit easier for me to investigate inequality and I think they made me a better reporter, too. I was aided as a journalist by my public-school education in one obvious way. Whilst it didn't do me much good academically, I left those institutions confident and independent. I like people. I'm a people person, no question. And having formative experiences when I met people who were very different from me, who lived in a very different part of the world or had experienced a very different life, was an enormous privilege. I loved every second of it. When I then came to journalism in my early thirties, it was like coming home – I was able to meet more people, many of them very different to myself, and help tell their stories.

My route to journalism, then, was circuitous. But my drive to succeed once there was very direct. This drive came from the fact that everybody in my family was convinced that I was A) thick and B) therefore destined for mediocrity. I was determined to prove them wrong. I was also determined to prove that theirs was not the only way to progress. Their way involved a great deal of hard work at school, which I was completely incapable of, and a good deal of academic smarts, which I seemed to be utterly lacking. My father was a bishop, and headmaster of a public school. I had two very bright brothers either side of me. Amongst these two shining lights of intelligence and culture, I was the thicko in the middle. But my mother was a brilliant pianist, and from her I developed a love of music. As a child, I had a good singing voice; it won me a scholarship to a choristers' school.

There's nothing like being a chorister in an ancient cathedral singing the most extraordinary and beautiful music. In my case, the aesthetics in Winchester Cathedral were unbelievable. Not just the music, but the Norman architecture, with huge arches giving way to the flying buttresses of the Gothic period. I loved working with the other choristers, being a part of something bigger than ourselves. Even singing with the basses, who were often men many years my senior, alongside the organist and the choirmaster was often a joy. It was a very diverse set of personalities and types who came together to make something lovely. It was like being in the army, really, albeit a very choice army. What I learnt at the choristers' school wasn't Latin, it wasn't French, it wasn't even elementary maths. I learnt how to articulate, to use my voice to its absolute fullest extreme. I learnt how to operate in a team intersecting with twenty other voices to produce the most ethereal consequences. These two things, a desire to prove myself and my years as a chorister, in a very strange way prepared me to read Channel 4 News. I was also, of course, lucky to have come of age in a time when a posh accent seemed to tack a few points on to your IQ score.

As I said, it's not the way my parents would have expected me to get there, and indeed it's not the way most of my colleagues did. But, given my own unconventional route, I am passionate about supporting people into the newsroom today who perhaps don't have the right grades, or the right school, or the right social polish. A good journalist likes people, knows how to work with and for them, has a nose for a story and the drive to make sure that it's *their* story that's leading the programme that night. You can't teach those things easily, they're instinctual, and there are plenty of double firsts from Cambridge who don't have them. A society with lots of inequality will never be able to offer opportunities to people who don't sit neatly in a certain box. An unequal society sets up people who are different, in whatever way, to fail.

The future of us

As any journalist knows, when you're living in the period that you're talking about it's very hard to stand back and be sure of what is actually happening. Having said that, whilst some of the facts and figures around inequality suggest that things are getting worse, intuitively, there are aspects that, whilst harder to measure, are undoubtedly getting better. This is important, because if things got better in the past, we should feel convinced that, with effort, they can continue to improve. It's not a straight line. It's not inevitable. And certainly, the fact that things have improved is no excuse for us to rest on our laurels. But we should know that our efforts to make a better society are not wasted.

For instance, state education is significantly better than

it was in the 1950s. I think there's plenty of evidence, particularly with the expansion of university education, that a lot of progress has been made in terms of opportunity. Nevertheless, so long as the market is skewed by the rarefied provision of private education, it will be very hard to battle inequality on that front. Likewise, equality between the genders is markedly different today in comparison to the 1950s. Women are better educated, are more integrated in the workplace, and have greater financial independence than when I first entered the workforce; but there remains an intolerable gender pay gap. Moreover, women are still too often the victims of male violence. Finally, in my lifetime, we have gone from being a chauvinist imperial power to a much more tolerant multicultural society. However, the fact that the highest-profile group agitating for equality between races must call themselves 'Black Lives Matter' tells us that we have a very long road ahead of us. The shocking statistics[6] that we saw during the Covid-19 pandemic – with ethnic minorities experiencing worse outcomes in every field than the white majority – clearly show that we have not yet arrived at any kind of racial end point. Typically, liberals in the UK have smugly wagged their finger at US police brutality or American educational outcomes. But the protests led by Black Lives Matter that emerged following the murder of George Floyd expressed the many ways in which racial inequities, right here in the UK, are far from being solved.

Historically, I think the biggest problem is that people

haven't been prepared to talk about the issues of inequality in blunt terms. We've been afraid to call it what it is. I'm quite sure that the word inequality turns up much more now than it ever did when I was a child and that, in and of itself, is an achievement. We used to think the world looked like it did for no apparent reason – it was just a fact of life. We are more questioning of authority today.

And yet Grenfell thrust inequality straight in our faces. Things may have improved, but we're not there yet. In fact, we have a long way to go. Worse still, in difficult economic times – and we are living through yet another phase of difficult times, exacerbated by war and plague – progress has a tendency to stall. There was progress, I don't think we can deny that. But now we appear to be going backwards.

It is hard to say definitively why this is happening. To some extent, I believe that not enough people in positions of authority are battling against inequality. Thinking back to the time before I was born, the birth of the welfare state, the development of the NHS, the reform of our educational institutions were enormous moments which had a profound impact on inequality and were ultimately due to political will from both major political parties. It is an inescapable truth that living conditions and education and welfare have vastly improved in my lifetime. Since this explosion, though, we have seen some tinkering, but no major initiative that has struck a significant blow against inequality. Taking the long view, since 1945 it seems to me that the state has done quite a good job of working at inequality. Progress has slowed in the last twenty or thirty years, but it's the state that has made the biggest dent. To quote directly from the Equality Trust:

> The UK became a much more equal nation during the post-war years. The data available shows that the share of income going to the top 10 per cent of the population fell over the 40 years to 1979, from 34.6 per cent in 1938 to 21 per cent in 1979, while the share going to the bottom 10 per cent rose slightly.
>
> Since 1979 this process of narrowing inequality has reversed sharply . . . Inequality rose considerably over the 1980s, reaching a peak in 1990. Since 2010, income shares have been relatively unchanged.[7]

The reason for the post-war equality was not that manna from heaven magically rained down; it is that, after the Second World War, we, the people, took the decision to look after each other. Howard Glennerster from the London School of Economics parsed the data. He writes: 'In 1937 social policy reduced overall inequality by about a quarter. The post-war welfare state in 1948 reduced the, by then, more equal original market incomes by nearly a half – almost twice as much as in 1937. Despite the growing inequality in original incomes since then, social policy has continued to reduce inequality.'[8] That's why I say that it's the state that has had the biggest impact, and it is to the state that we must look in the future.

Inequality persists. Our welfare state has suffered significant damage. And there are enormous challenges involved in accessing the benefits of the private sector and spreading them evenly; inequality rages in that sector, and the fundamentals of the class system are still present.

And yet we should feel optimistic about our ability to turn things around. I was born in the same year as the National Health Service. To this day, the NHS is a remarkably class-free, cohesive provision. Of course, there are breakdowns. There are moments when it doesn't do quite as well as one would hope. But in general it's an absolutely amazing resource and I think we are, rightly, immensely proud of it. Woe betide any politician who decides to campaign against it; the only reason for so doing is to deny the health service money, ensuring the elite can use the tax they save to buy the services we currently get for free. I doubt the people of Britain will accept that. Everything has its problems but, taken all for all, the NHS is pretty damn good. It took a long time to come about: from that wonderful initial commitment it's taken decades to get where it is now, but through hard work and a shared ethic between people of different ideologies we brought it into being.

We have every chance of extending this ethic to other areas of our social lives. Political parties are not good at collaborating, and there are people on both the right and left who will never work together, even though they share more of each other's view than they may think.

Nevertheless, despite our supposed ideological divides, we still have an established welfare state, an established state education system and an established NHS. Any government which withers health, education or social provision will suffer greatly in the long run. Over twelve years of Tory rule, despite large cuts, these bodies have not been stripped to the bone. Given that mortality rates continue to go down, and life expectancy (until 2020, when the pandemic skewed things) continues to rise, it would be hard to argue that the health of our nation is generally getting worse.[9] Clearly, though, progress is slowing – it may be stalling – and we run the risk of it reversing. If it does, expect to see some very nervous Tory MPs come election time.

A more equal society is possible. Even in recent memory the welfare state and social housing afforded people a right to live a decent life. The agreement to build a society based on a communitarian ethic used to be uncontroversial for both of the two main parties. That world seems very far away now, and even looking back to it seems an odd exercise when longing for the past is monopolized by Brexiteers. I don't have any particular nostalgia – it's in the nature of society to evolve and to have ups and downs. In general, I look forward to better times and I remain optimistic about our future. In my view, most of the things which go wrong can be rectified and will be rectified. That belief has always driven me as a journalist. I think that if you believe nothing can be done, you'll end up a very unhappy individual.

Progress is precious; we owe it to each other to continue the hard work of making it happen. For my part, I've always believed that it is a journalist's job to ensure that people have enough information to understand that something can be done, and that from there it is in their hands.

And so the bitterness that I feel about Grenfell is caused by an admission of an awful truth: their fate wasn't in their own hands. It was in the hands of people who would never live in a tower block like that, let alone begin to understand the conditions of those who do.

Desperately, I learnt the truth of Firdaws' last hours just days after seeing her image pasted to a wall outside the blackened Grenfell Tower. She, along with her whole family, had been incinerated. Their remains were identified using DNA. It breaks my heart, *absolutely breaks my heart*, every time I think of her.

Had she lived, what were Firdaws' chances of reaching the peak of any profession? It would have been tough, but I think she had the power and intelligence to break through. Our collective neglect denied her even that slender chance. Her death seems to me to sum up the absolute core of what the fire at Grenfell Tower was about and what, by extension, this book is about. It is indeed about the outrageousness of inequality. It is about aspiration and ability, cut off at an incredibly young age. It is about a gut feeling of unfairness. Her death sums up everything that is wrong with inequality and everything that we must guard against.

Nothing is fixed: journalism is about ensuring that people understand that. So too is this book. I am not aiming to dictate solutions to you, the reader; I wish only to inform you that you have the power in your hands. If a lesson is to come from Grenfell, it will come from ensuring that people understand what happened, and what they need to do to safeguard against it happening again. That means voting out local councils or national politicians when they show themselves to lack commitment on tackling inequality. It means pressuring your councillors and MPs to deliver services that should be taken for granted. And it means investing in your community – whether that means volunteering at a homeless shelter, or simply making a point to talk to your neighbours.

After the prize was given, there was a video taken of Firdaws which you can still see on YouTube.[10] Looking confidently beyond the camera at the interviewer, she says, with winning charm, 'I enjoyed [the debate competition] so much. It was such an amazing experience meeting Bill Gates, winning a Nando's voucher, and I want to thank everyone that contributed towards it . . . Being involved [was] fun, amazing and interesting, because it gives you a voice to say what you think, to say what you believe, to help change the world.'

We owe it to Firdaws to give others like her a voice, to

say what they think, to say what they believe and to help them change the world. That's why I have written this book. That's the purpose of journalism and, by extension, of my career so far. And that's the prize on offer to a society that tackles inequality at the root.

CHAPTER 2

THE OLD WAYS

MY FATHER WAS ENORMOUS. He stood about seven foot six when wearing his bishop's mitre, and a colossal six foot six in his civvies. I never considered following his size 13 shoes into the Church. To this day I haven't developed a settled view about God, and I certainly don't lie in bed at night thinking about it. But as a boy, I loved all that went with it – the music, the camaraderie, the architecture and even, perhaps especially, the dressing up.

Beyond his ecclesiastical duties he was headmaster of Ardingly College. This was quite a common situation. Many of our public schools have religious foundations. Ardingly was part of a group called the Woodard Schools, founded in the mid-nineteenth century by the priest Nathaniel Woodard. Their basis was 'sound principle and sound knowledge, firmly grounded in the Christian faith'. By the time my father was headmaster, the faith-based grounding was a little less firm than it had been a hundred years previously – Christian pageantry and ethics endured, but they weren't quite at the centre of school life. On the other hand, the sense of a class system was an inheritance that remained central and unchecked. The students all came from the same social milieu and were destined for bourgeois life. They did not express an interest in becoming miners or factory workers, and nobody seriously expected that it was a possibility that they would take up those traditionally working-class roles. Class was an invisible hand that guided the boys' futures.

We would go to Ardingly's chapel every Sunday. It was in the middle of Sussex, very rural. One day I noticed an unhappy-looking man sitting at the other end of our pew. He seemed old, with saggy eyebrows, and he wore an oversized greatcoat. At the end of the service my father introduced me.

'Jonathan,' for that was what he called me, 'This is Mr Harold Macmillan. He is the prime minister.'

Macmillan chimed in, 'Do you know what a prime minister is, young man?'

I was still in single figures, eight or so, I should think. 'Are you married to the Queen?' I said to him.

He chortled and said, 'Oh, no, no, no, no. I'm a Conservative politician, and I run the country.'

In that exchange, I derived a sense of the hierarchy that is Britain. 'I run the country' is a very possessive description of his job. I don't blame Macmillan – I think he was speaking in shorthand. He merely thought, 'How can I tell this little idiot what I do?' And it came out as 'I run the country.' His saggy eyebrow told me that running the country didn't seem to have made him very happy. It was difficult to take this thought further at the time. I was very young, and it is hard to question whether things are normal or right when they are all that you know.

My father himself had gone to Winchester. He was steeped in the whole public-school set-up. He thought public schools were a good institution: they bred good boys (because women were not allowed back then) into good men. He thought that their upshot – class – was a good thing too; I certainly never heard him criticizing it, though quite how the class system was compatible with my father's Christianity, I didn't know. Each week he would sermonize on the fundamentals of the religion: love thy neighbour as thy brother. The meek shall inherit the earth. Whoever is generous to the poor lends to the Lord. As I grew older, I began to sense that there was something in these values that contrasted with my father's assumptions about how our society ought to work.

Our relationship was of a piece with the relationships boys had with their fathers back then. He was from a different age, and it made him a difficult person to be fond of. He was remote, and I liked it that way. As a child, on my way to bed, I would pass his open study door and say goodnight – no kisses. He was busy working on yet another sermon. I detected from an early age that his life was perfect and complete without having to take too much notice of me. Still, he was a kindly old boy, and we rarely argued, whereas my elder brother, who is a radical trade unionist, was completely the opposite. There was plenty of fire at the dining table, and occasionally even some brimstone.

I wouldn't say I was close to my father then, but I was very fond of my mother. She could play Brahms to die for. But poor Mum lost all her hair to alopecia, which struck when she was a vulnerable teenager. It brutally undermined her confidence to play in public, even though her wigs were, to me, extremely convincing – indeed, so convincing were they that I was at least eight years old before I discovered her secret. My father managed to crash his eccentric car, an open-top Hudson Terraplane 8 that had starred in the 1930 New York Motor Show. He tipped it over on a sharp bend in a Sussex lane and my mother was thrown out of the car and scarred on the head. My parents decided they had better tell us about the alopecia in case the crash led to us finding out anyway. I think that because of her alopecia my mother depended on me emotionally in a way that my father never did. My mother required my attentiveness and care. Father didn't really need anything; as far as he was concerned he had his life sorted. But my mother needed me more, and I enjoyed helping her – most of us enjoy helping others. We were close.

It was she who discovered I could sing. My parents concluded that the best thing to do with me was to get me into a good cathedral choir. My father recognized that if I got into the choir, I'd get a free private education – a private education being essential, and a free one being a bonus. Having gone to Winchester College, he decided Winchester Cathedral was the place for me to be. My mother trained me up for the voice trials that would qualify me (or not) for entry. Through my mother's good instruction, I managed to win a place. Off I went.

The choir school had about eighty pupils. My number was seventy-eight. I had probably just managed to squeak in. It was nice walking to the cathedral every day to sing, but besides that there were no films or slide shows or lectures or anything that might have cheered the place up. When we weren't singing or in our normal lessons, there was nothing much to do. We spent a lot of time walking across the Close, the nexus around the cathedral, to get to choir practice or to go to the services. We did this in a snake, two by two by two. This ritual was very important; it was also very weird. Not many people snake around a place, but we did, and we did very little else. I was lucky, though, because singing made me happy. It has done all my life; music is important to me. It's not very compatible with journalism, unfortunately, but I still sing in the bath.

I was thirteen when I went to my big school, which was in Oxford. What is there to say about it beyond the fact that it was a very odd place to be an adolescent? There was quite a lot of innuendo, or worse, in terms of older boys wanting to get off with younger boys. At the time, this was the hallmark of every public school: you couldn't conceivably put a whole lot of adolescent boys together in the absence of any girls and be entirely sure that there wouldn't be any sexual activity. Ask anybody of my age who went to public school and they will almost certainly agree that this was the case.

I felt as though public school was something of an act. People were trying to be posh. Of course, they were posh, but they were performing it too. They were trying to be . . . honestly, I don't know what they were trying to be. But my overwhelming feeling is that we adolescent boys were not existing in our natural state. They talk about public school 'shaping' you, and that's what it felt like, as though we were being pressed into a shape, like a component on an assembly line. The school imposed ludicrous traditions and a culture on us, including its own vocabulary. There were no changing rooms, only 'chaggers'. Its hierarchy was designed around prefects who were empowered to impose punishments of one sort or another. All of it was designed to consolidate the school's culture. It was an old institution and we were being institutionalized by it.

Public school did little for me academically, despite the many promises made to parents to induce them to part with cash. I left with nothing by way of academic credentials, and I needed to get some if I was going to go to university. It was at this moment that my life changed irrevocably.

To scrape together some A-Levels, I was sent to Scarborough Technical College. This was a completely different experience to anything I had been brought up with. And I *loved* it. What an absolute feast! First, there were masses of young women. Until this point I'd had no contact with women except for my mother, my nanny and the odd Swiss au pair – I was eighteen years old. Admittedly, it was a little overwhelming. I attempted to do a shorthand and typing course and turned out to be the only boy in the forty-student class. I just couldn't cope, I was too shy. But for the first time in my life I had friends who were women, and it was a revelation.

So much surprised me about the lives of my new friends. I had led such a sheltered existence that I had never given a thought to how people from other backgrounds lived. The public school was a monastery, so cloistered and unrepresentative of the world beyond. It came to me as both a joy and a relief to discover a whole new world. Life outside the buttoned-up institutions I'd been a part of was, overall, far more organic-feeling. But I was surprised, too, by many new realities I had to confront. The fulfilment of other people's ambitions was stunted by the institutional structures around them, more than I had ever witnessed before. I was also surprised to find how much more hand-to-mouth life was and that in every dimension, physical and social, those less privileged had far less mobility.

Also, I'd never been to a pub in my life. I'd never drunk alcohol. Suddenly, I realized money didn't always go very far. You had to be a bit careful about how many drinks ended up being in your round. The pubs were rather smoky, but talking to people wasn't a problem, even though I had a posh accent. 'Jon bloody Snow,' I would hear, 'where the hell have you come from?' I got plenty of that, but it was good-natured and easy to cope with. After all, you can't but admit that a public school does foster a kind of independence that enables you to deal with more or less any situation. In retrospect I can see that I had been tutored to enable me to prosper in Britain's class system – I was taught to think of myself as a leader, not a follower. This wasn't the same as being taught that class mattered. It didn't matter to us, because it was made clear that we were destined for the upper classes.

Because of that, a private education puts up barriers. It marks you out as different, not least because of that posh accent the regulars in the pub ribbed me for. Here, though, for the first time I found my barriers coming down. The pub was a community. It was fun to go, have a drink, and get along with people. The same was true with women. I had met very few people of a different class to me, and never in such an informal and equal setting. I found out that I liked people who hadn't been privately educated. At the college, too, my fellow students were a real mix of people. But their backgrounds didn't matter – I made friends easily.

It even started to look like I might cobble together an A-Level or two. The staff were lovely. I found it completely extraordinary to be taught by people who were at peace with themselves; the public-school teachers, in a funny sort of way, never were. At the tech, I didn't feel that people were putting on any sort of act. But at the public school everybody, particularly the teachers, was aspiring to be something more than they were. That was true for me, too. Suddenly, there was no pressure to be something I wasn't; I was free of all that.

It was wonderful. Just wonderful. I felt a kind of social ease, and for the first time I was relaxed and comfortable in my own skin. Above all, as I was realizing, things here were much more normal. I hadn't known what normality was until I encountered Scarborough Technical College and suddenly I was thrust into everyday life with everyday people. I liked it, and I liked them, substantially more than the isolated, chilly, rarefied world that I had come from.

It was wonderful, for the first time, just to *be*.

Institutions and their discontents

My father was shaped by institutions – the Church and the private-school system. The upshot was that he believed in another British institution: the class system. At root, the class system tells us that we are different from each other. It says that Lord Such and Such is 'above' Mr So and So. This is a lie. We're not different to each other, and we certainly shouldn't form our opinions about each other because of the vagaries of what our great-grandparents did. Still, such institutions shape us, and shape our society.

This chapter is about old British institutions and how they operate today. I am a product of the private-school system and, to a lesser extent, the Anglican Church, and I have dealt with other institutions in my working life – large media companies, and the two Houses of Parliament. Above all I have seen the problems and inequalities caused by what many of these lesser institutions help to establish: the class system. Perhaps it feels curiously anachronistic to talk about the British class system – the political debate of our age often seems to overlook it. And yet where you were born, what your parents did and where you went to school still play an enormous role in what you yourself end up doing with your life. Not talking about class only serves the class system's beneficiaries.

I'm going to use this chapter to explain why I think some of these institutions look creaky in modern Britain and may require renewal. We take it as given today that people are born equal, but that wasn't the assumption at the time when many of our national institutions – like the education system and Parliament – were created. Without any modern intervention, we get the same old system of class divisions we claim to have left behind. But I also want to explain why I think some institutions are important. Chiefly, they foster community. I loved the choir for its camaraderie and shared purpose. There are other values, like brotherhood or learning or even collective support in times of grief, that our institutions can nurture in us. On the other hand, as in public schools, a close-knit community can be aloof from the wider populace within which it exists. Institutions exist to foster community, but unfortunately they sometimes end up doing just the opposite: hospitals that fail Black mothers, newspapers that ignore the poor, governments that promote a politician's own interest rather than the public good. Clearly, our educational institutions should tear down barriers between people and provide equal opportunities for all, but they have been captured over the years, and barriers have become entrenched.

Besides helping me to scrape together a C, D and an E at A-Level, Scarborough Tech taught me a valuable lesson, one that is really, in my view, the key to the whole business of being a human being. The object of life is the ability to live harmoniously with others. I'd glimpsed it in a choir, and even, through the cracks, at my other schools, but suddenly there it was in primary colours at Scarborough Tech. I didn't articulate it like this at the time; all I knew was that I was happy there in a way that I had not been anywhere else.

For me to truly understand that the importance of living harmoniously with others, I had to leave Britain behind entirely.

At the age of eighteen I followed up Scarborough Tech with Voluntary Service Overseas in Uganda, where I was to teach young people. If Scarborough Tech was a big jump for me after my sheltered and isolated childhood, Uganda was a quantum leap!

I'd never been out of Britain. I'd never been on an aeroplane. I had very little experience of meeting people who were not white. As I stepped off the plane I was, for the first time, an ethnic minority. And from that moment on, I was bombarded with experiences the likes of which I'd never had before. It was a terrific adventure.

I was picked up from the airport by the headmaster, a Catholic cleric. He was British, and a rather austere character, a sort I was familiar with. He contrasted starkly with all the unfamiliar things around me on that first journey to the school. It was green for a start. I mean, unbelievably green – a lush colour that we simply don't see in England. And it was hot, hot, *hot*, probably 90 or 95 degrees Fahrenheit (over 30 Celsius). The rudimentary airport, the second airport I'd ever seen, was quite a contrast from the first: Heathrow. Heathrow was all concrete and glass. Here, the buildings were roofed with corrugated iron. We travelled along the banks of the Nile – if you're going to go to Uganda, you want to be on the banks of the Nile. It is bliss, a landscape for which there are no words. And, of course, the road we travelled on had no tarmac. We were on murram roads, beaten-clay roads, very red, which contrasted beautifully with the bright-green hinterland.

When we arrived, I discovered that the school was fifteen miles from the nearest shop or even postbox. My mother wrote to me every week, and the only way to get her letters was to travel that distance. But it was the school itself which was the greatest discovery of all. It was absolutely fantastic. On what felt like the other side of the world, in a place so different from where I had come from, I discovered the thing I had been looking for – a wonderful community of boys and girls. Most were of a pretty similar age to me, seventeen, eighteen or nineteen, and we got on superbly. There was one other VSO, and a smattering of priests and staff. In all there were fewer than a dozen British people and over 500 Ugandans. Having no prior experience, I found teaching a trial. I'd call myself academically challenged at that time, and I was suddenly teaching others who were virtually only a page behind me in the book. Not only that, but I was also teaching *everything* – English, geography, history, you name it. I'd been thrown in at the deep end.

Whilst, particularly at the start, I wasn't sure I was the best teacher, I loved the routine and regimen of the school. There was a rigid timetable of events and rituals, starting every morning by raising the flag and singing, 'Uganda, the land of freedom, we lay our future in thy hands. United we, for liberty together we will always stand.' Our version only had one verse and we would often sing it several times, but it was sung every day. Lessons would run after this and then, outside of school hours, we would go and fish in the Nile. Though the current was rather ferocious, we would paddle about near the shore, oblivious to the reality that there were occasionally crocodiles and hippopotami. All in all, it was the greatest experience I could have wished for, and without a doubt it set my life on a different course.

Crucially, as mentioned, I hadn't met many Black people prior to going to Uganda. The public-school system was designed to make you feel different to others, which breeds a kind of ill-ease in their company. But I came back to Britain totally at ease with everybody. A year in Uganda caused me to realize that race was, in essence, a nonsense – the colour of my skin and that of another person's skin was not a legitimate point of difference between us; there were far more salient ones. For instance, plenty of those young people were more academic than I was. I couldn't avoid knowing this, because I was doing my best to teach them and, frankly, they deserved better. Which led inevitably to a realization of the most crucial point of difference: I had opportunities that they did not because of where I had been born, and who my parents had been. I knew it to be a grotesque unfairness and I felt miserable that my new friends had been denied the same chances as me.

But in Uganda I also saw a kind of possibility. I had discovered for myself that you could forge a community with people who were from a very different background to yours. If you throw five complete strangers from anywhere in the world into a room with each other, there are always commonalities between them. I knew it was possible to look beyond the barriers erected by the institutions I had been a part of. And I saw the immense value of the communities that could be created when you did.

After Uganda, I returned to Britain with the belief that any institution that tried to uphold a false division, such as race, was ludicrous. Unfortunately, I then found myself in one: Liverpool University.

I should preface this by saying that I only got in because my father met a professor of law from the university on a train. By the end of the journey my father had persuaded him that he ought to take me on as a student. I had three very bad A-Levels in Economics, Law (helpfully) and English. I got English when I was at public school, and Economics and Law from Scarborough Tech. Unfortunately, the grades were not good enough to secure me a place anywhere. But, after my father's intervention, I was in at Liverpool and studying Law, a subject it turned out I had no interest in whatsoever.

In 1971 Liverpool University was alive with discussion about apartheid and Mandela. You could certainly say that it was already a multicultural university: there were a lot of Black and Asian students alongside white students, and so the conversations about South Africa were already in full flow. It was the dawning of the Mandela age. I don't think many people in the UK knew who he was until roughly that sort of time, even though he had suffered gravely long before that. The seeds had been sown for me in Uganda. Though I was only dimly aware of the apartheid struggle, I had grown acutely conscious of the inequalities and disparities between the Global North and South more generally. Sympathy for the anti-apartheid cause was natural for me.

In circles that grew out of more parochial student politics, we started looking for a Liverpool angle, one that would galvanize local people and show that, whilst the struggle was far away, we were all connected. Such a link was not hard to find. We had a very inappropriate individual as chancellor of the university: the Marquess of Salisbury. He had utterly antediluvian views, which he expressed loudly in the House of Lords. Salisbury was a dyed-in-the-wool imperialist. For instance, when Seretse Khama, who would go on to be the first president of Botswana, married a white Englishwoman in England, Salisbury campaigned to have Khama remain in England, so dangerous a precedent did he think it would set if he were to return to Africa with a white wife. Throughout the 1960s, Salisbury was vociferous in his support of the apartheid government of South Africa and, undoubtedly, was a convinced and committed white supremacist. Yet Liverpool University was a multicultural community; to have somebody in authority with such extreme views was inappropriate and offensive.

We concluded that our small contribution to the anti-apartheid struggle should be an attempt to get rid of him. We had little say in the matter, but we felt we should demonstrate against his being the chancellor, and there followed lots of mass meetings, rallies and assemblies. Eventually we heard that he was coming up on the train to officiate at some university event. It fell to me, because I had a posh voice, to go to Liverpool Lime Street, meet the train that he was arriving on, and tell him that his presence at the university would be undesirable.

As he stepped on to the platform, I collared him. 'My Lord,' I said. 'My name is Jon Snow. I've been sent here on behalf of the Students' Union to tell you that a vote has been taken, and carried by very large majority, declaring that we feel that it would be better if you were not the chancellor.'

Surprisingly, he responded quite calmly: 'Very well. I shan't come any further then. I shall return to my home. I never liked coming here in the first place. And I shall never come here again.' With that he got on the next train back to London, and that was the end of him. It was an extraordinary moment. I think we were naïve enough to imagine that this was a natural consequence of a campaign we believed to be entirely justified – nevertheless, it was pints all round at the student pub soon after. Today I look back and think we didn't really understand the gravity of our achievement – defenestrating one of the top lords in the land. It was a great coup for my first attempt at holding the powerful to account, albeit one aided by hundreds of other students.

Of course, the authorities were at their wits' end: they'd got a lord and then they'd lost him. They were scandalized. His was, after all, an important name on the notepaper, and these oiks, these creeps, these *students* got it into their heads to make him go. It didn't go down at all well. They chucked out those of us who were most closely associated with getting rid of Salisbury, me included. I could have gone back; I think I was rusticated for two years. But I didn't want to. I had already begun to live another life.

By this time, I had been persuaded that Liverpool University, and institutions in general, were not inherently right. In fact, they get things wrong all the time. Having said this, I could also see that institutions had a powerful role to play in our society, because they helped us to create communities. A university is a great example – Liverpool University was, after all, a fantastic, multicultural community whilst I was there, and this campus culture wouldn't have happened if the institution had not existed in the first place. We need institutions. But we need them to have the flexibility to renew themselves, reflecting and serving the communities they represent.

At the time, Liverpool University was unable to renew itself; it was stuck clinging to a past that would very quickly recede in the rear-view mirror. It had become incapable of serving the needs of its community and had even grown actively offensive to that community. In a case like this, the institution is fighting a losing battle: it can only gain legitimacy through effective service to its community and loses that legitimacy when it uses its power to institutionalize division. As time went by, fewer and fewer people wanted to be associated with apartheid South Africa, and the university was forced to reflect that in its policies.

Apartheid was institutionalized racism pure and simple. A community – South Africa – made up of different ethnicities, had divisions enforced by the institutions of state: the courts, the legislature, the police, the armed forces. Powerful, unaccountable institutions were wheeled out to administer the divide in the community, driving person from person and creating the most dreadful inequality we can imagine.

When I got chucked out of Liverpool University, today's reality in South Africa seemed a very distant dream. Lord Salisbury was not the only person in the 1960s who thought apartheid was worth protecting. Indeed, Margaret Thatcher's government was, as late as 1987, calling the African National Congress 'terrorists'. That same year, she said that anyone who believed the ANC would ever rule South Africa was 'living in cloud-cuckoo-land'.[1] And yet Nelson Mandela led the ANC to victory in South Africa's first ever free election with full enfranchisement just seven years later. This is not to say that South Africa has turned into a utopia. But, with time and much effort, apartheid has been destroyed.

When institutions become intransigent, when they don't meet the needs of the people, tensions build. In the case of South Africa, these tensions were made manifest by the bravery of those many anti-apartheid campaigners – Mandela chief amongst them – who were willing to put their freedom, and even their lives, on the line. When we challenge institutions all around the world, we would do well to remember that even some of the most powerful ones have, in the recent past, changed beyond recognition.

Political institutions in Britain today

Thankfully, we don't face anything like apartheid here in Britain. But over time, all institutions get creaky and need to be renewed by the community that founded them, otherwise all kinds of inequalities begin to creep in. In certain of our political institutions, that feels very much the case today.

Westminster is an intimidating place. I find it intimidating even though I've been going in and out of it for forty years. I've never felt I belong there. I don't feel I have any right to be there, although I do because I'm a journalist. It's true that, because of my background, I am less likely to feel intimidated by giant doors, ancient vaulted ceilings and esoteric codes of conduct. But the fact is, I do feel intimidated, and it's not a place where your average Joe would want to pop in and see what's going on. In many respects that's a great pity: the House of Commons exists to represent the interests of the average Joe. If the public feel unwelcome there, how can they feel assured that their interests are well represented?

I don't have all the answers. I am, after all, a hack, not a constitutional expert. But at the very least, I think we need to analyse what makes it intimidating. So much of our politics is steeped in ancient history, but how much of that helps the place's purpose? Does knowing who is an Honourable Member and who is a Right Honourable Member make you a more effective politician? Does saying prayers whilst facing a wall before Parliament begins improve accountability? Is it useful that endorsements to Bills sent from the House of Lords to the House of Commons are written in Norman French?[2] I would say in all conscience that anybody who wants to change, and hopefully improve, the way the country is governed should immediately set up a proper constitutional review of *how* we're governed. At the moment, a lot of things aren't particularly clear.

Let's take just one example. In general, I think that dispersing power – what is sometimes called devolution – is a good thing. There may well be significant powers unique to Westminster – on housing, say, or healthcare spending – which would be much better devolved to a local authority. But I'm not sure, because I'm still not, in truth, totally sure which powers reside with which part of government, and I don't imagine very many people are. I certainly don't think the powers that reside with central and local government are there because somebody went through an intensive reviewing process and figured out the most efficient way for power to be distributed through the country. The last time there was any significant wholesale reform of local government was in 1972.[3] Much has changed since then. Are the powers that local government has the right ones? What should their impact be, for example, on the local health system, on the care system, on mental health? There must be aspects of policy in which local government is much better versed than central government because it is closer to the people who actually use the services; but what they are specifically is very hard to say without properly reviewing the state we are already in.

I think it's uncontroversial to say that it would be a good thing if a career in politics was more accessible to a greater variety of people: I believe that representation is the key to change for the better. Having said that, it's already becoming a surprisingly wide pool of people. Wales and Scotland have reasonably democratic outcomes and Westminster has become much more representative in my working lifetime. It does not yet reflect the ethnic, class or gender make-up of the country, but it has come a long way. 'In 2019, 65 MPs were from minority ethnic backgrounds, 10 per cent of the total. This was an increase of 25 per cent compared to 52 in 2017. In contrast, there were 4 minority ethnic MPs elected in 1987.'[4] The 10 per cent of 2019 did not reflect the 15 per cent minority ethnic composition of the population – so, some way to go, but there has been positive movement since the late 1980s. And, whilst they get a bad rap, there are some excellent people in the House of Commons from across the political spectrum, and from a diversity of backgrounds. Besides that, like it or not, the Commons is democratically elected, therefore I'm loath to question the electorate's decisions. When the public voted for Thatcher, they got her. When they voted for Blair, they got him. It's the same with your local MP. You aren't lumbered with an MP who knows nothing of local concerns and local people – you can kick them out. It's true that, at the present time, many politicians are pulled from the professions, or go direct from PPE at Oxford into a political role. But, with time, due to the democratic mechanism, I have faith that the make-up of the House of Commons will slowly come to represent the communities that it is drawn from.

The process hasn't been quick and still has a way to go.

To accelerate it, I suspect that the best thing to do would be to move the Houses of Parliament out of Westminster and into another part of the country – the Midlands being the most obvious candidate. There are all kinds of reasons for this; chief amongst them is that it would allow MPs to spend more time in the constituencies they are supposed to represent, and less time in the so-called 'Westminster bubble'. Equally, a building that doesn't look like a medieval fortress and is situated in a place that's geographically accessible to greater numbers of people is inherently more user-friendly than the current set-up. It's hardly a panacea, but it would go some way to easing that feeling of intimidation I've spoken about.

There are other circumstances of Westminster that, to some extent, dampen our politics. There are interests in play which are not strictly about the matter in hand, and they are often difficult to define or pin down. They might be linked to class or ethnicity, they might be any of the things which have become such critical issues in our society – even extending to the corporate interests which employ or consult Members of Parliament. My sense down the years is that race, sex and class have all played a significant role in our politics, and politicians have actively tolerated, if not actively supported, many of the divisions in our society. Does the legislature adequately take account of these facts? I think it doesn't, particularly when it comes to the House of Lords. The Commons strikes me as essentially democratic, but the Lords is definitely not. The house of review cannot do its job properly if it doesn't perform at least as well as the lower house in representing the people. Currently, the House of Lords contains a hereditary element, and this should be insupportable in a modern democracy. The Lords, therefore, is the institution most obviously ripe for renewal.

I don't think anybody sees the House of Lords as perfect, and there have been attempts to do something about it. The argument has been going on for my entire lifetime. Indeed, the aforementioned Lord Salisbury, when he wasn't defending the apartheid regime of South Africa, spent much time defending the ability of the House of Lords to prevent new legislation passing.[5] The House of Lords holds less sway now than then, but nothing truly significant has changed and there must be a better way of doing it.

At the same time, I recognize how hard it is to commit to such a giant reform. For one thing, as a general rule the British people are small-c 'conservative' and don't like big changes. I don't think it's a good idea to have a nominated House of Lords. There are drawbacks with prime ministerial appointment, and I don't believe it's wise to have a chamber of review that is in some way in competition with the main chamber – you don't want to denude the latter of its capacity to govern. It's very difficult in a democracy to have two chambers, both fully democratically elected: that way must lie some degree of conflict. But on the other hand, having lived and worked in the United States, I think that the balance between Congress and Senate actually can work quite well, though it may not look like it at the moment. I would feel happier with that sort of a set-up, but the responsibilities there are very clearly delineated. It would be difficult to achieve something similar here.

Still, having said all that, and making clear that I don't profess to hold some magical solution to this problem, I can at the very least point out that an institution cannot be regarded as democratic if it simply involves a birth certificate. At the time of writing, there are four dukes, one marquess, twenty-five earls, seventeen viscounts, forty-four barons and two lords of Parliament amongst the ninety-two hereditary peers entitled to sit in the House of Lords. This is absolutely ridiculous. Anything which leads young people into believing that you can be born into power is very unwise. Anything that reeks of an inherent right to political power needs to go, and it needs to go fast. As for the Lords' hereditary element, it is pie in the sky; there should be no place for it in any part of our politics – it is an embarrassment and a nonsense. One final point on this is the overpopulation of our Upper House – it is second in size only to China's National People's Congress. Any process of modernization must also incorporate streamlining. So the House of Lords does need to be dealt with, firmly and quickly; to that end, I would support an independent commission to work out what would be the best solution. After all, the time has come to bring the Lords closer to any understanding of democracy.

My sense is that, just like Liverpool University, it is

inevitable that the House of Lords will change. It can't function effectively in a modern, democratic country if it retains a hereditary component. It will become incapable of serving our needs and, I believe, will seem increasingly offensive, anachronistic and irrelevant. Clinging blindly to tradition is always a losing game over the long haul. Change is difficult, but it also presents great opportunity; our politics suffers when it is not truly democratic and it will be improved by a reformed second chamber, one that provides effective, democratic scrutiny over the Commons.

Remembrance Sunday

In the Berkshire hamlet where I like to go with my family as often as we can, there is a tiny Norman church – cold as ice, and blessed with lovely stained glass, a wonky little pipe organ and uncomfortable pews. Today, sadly, the last full-time vicar – who looked after no fewer than six of these ancient establishments – has gone. Covid-19 ultimately ensured that there were, effectively, no longer many services.

However, when it came to marking Remembrance Sunday one recent November, those of us who live clustered around the church decided we would remedy matters. Even this tiny community lost loved ones and friends in war. More poignantly, this was the first Remembrance in the age of Covid-19. Some knew of victims in care homes, and some had friends or family fighting for their lives in hospital wards. Covid-19 had prompted certain members of our little community to pray as never before.

There were stringent 'lockdown' rules around meeting inside the church. So instead, we decided to set the service in the undulating sixteenth-century graveyard littered with ancient gravestones at wild angles. Flat paths would provide secure footings for those who required seating, and the soft grass between the graves was fine for the rest of us.

But who could lead the service? The size-13 shoes of my father, and his 'seven-foot-six-in-a-mitre' frame forced themselves into my mind's eye. Would it be sacrilege, I wondered. I thought of the twenty-five or so young soldiers from both wars whose names hung on a wooden plaque in the nave. They would *want* to be remembered. What was certain, too, was that many in our congregation wanted to take the opportunity to offer a prayer for the victims of the raging pandemic. And so it was that I, half unwittingly, became a temporary vicar. Someone rustled up a keyboard and sat it in the church porch. We thought maybe ten or twelve folks would come – but amazingly thirty-five of us made it to this remote churchyard that day.

Beyond my time as a chorister, never in my life had I officiated at a religious ceremony, let alone one to offer solace during the pandemic, and to remember the sacrifices of wartime. Never had I wanted to. All those family prayers with my father at breakfast time came flooding back. Those daily moments in which my parents stood at the dining table as I and my two brothers waited beside them, yearning for the Rice Krispies. Now, decades on, the ideas, the understanding and the responsibility, in this rustic setting, weighed heavily.

I summoned up my five years spent belting out hymns, psalms and anthems into the vast rafters of Winchester Cathedral. Somehow it all came together that Remembrance Sunday.

We've got a building. We've got candles. We've got somebody who can play the organ. But there isn't a priest, and that leaves our little village church in a sorry state. A lot of the explicitly religious components are no longer present, but what remains is a community, bonded by a shared set of values – in this case, thirty-five people who wanted to remember those who had passed, both recently and long ago. What I think is telling, and was expressed by our ersatz Remembrance Service, is that it's not the case that if there's no institution, there's no community. It's the other way around – if there's no community, there's no institution.

I spend almost none of my time thinking about God, but I think about community a lot. Institutions like village churches help grease a community's wheels. They provide a space for you to pull down barriers and get on with others, with perhaps also a shared commitment to a set of principles, like remembering fallen soldiers, or paying respects to lost loved ones together.

Despite my upbringing, the Church isn't a priority in

my life, and its potential today to establish communities is circumscribed. Much more important, I think, is politics. Politics is still the key when it comes to improving things for the community. For a community to flourish, it needs facilities, and they are often in the hands of politicians. There's a symbiotic relationship between the community and the institutions of political power which sometimes works and sometimes doesn't. What fascinates me, though, is that the community exists before the institution; most often, the institution forms out of the community. Take the origins of our schools – a community exists, it needs to educate its young, and it creates an institution to do it. Institutions exist to serve us; they should promote the flourishing of our communities. We don't exist to serve institutions, and institutions should never exclude or divide. Too often, we get things the wrong way around.

If there's a demand, it can be voiced and heard through institutions. Changing them is not always straightforward, and rarely is it easy, but the prize for doing so is something I discovered was the object of life at Scarborough Tech, and in Uganda, and in a little village church one Remembrance Sunday: to live harmoniously with others.

CHAPTER 3

WHERE WE LIVE

A new horizon

AFTER GETTING KICKED OUT OF Liverpool University, I was at a loss as to what to do. I was prepared to do more or less anything. So I put the word about that I needed a job, and that I wasn't too fussy.

My cousin, Peter Snow, had a friend who was secretary to the Earl of Longford, one of the most senior peers in the land, and known as both eccentric and a supporter of many causes. Through Peter I learnt that Longford was looking for somebody to run his day centre for homeless young people. As a matter of priority, they needed to find premises of their own – at the time they were in St Anne's Church in Soho. The role was about finding accommodation and doing admin rather than attending to the needs of the young people directly.

Interested, I went to meet Lord Longford to discuss the position. Amazingly, the other two trustees were there, too: Rear-Admiral Sir Matthew Slattery, and none other than John Profumo. At the time, Profumo was a controversial figure who had left Parliament accused of having had 'intimate relations' with a woman, Christine Keeler, who was alleged to be sleeping with a Soviet navy attaché. Profumo was also a delightfully eccentric figure committed to good works. Things were intriguing enough, before I'd even started working with any homeless people! After a quick chat, Longford appointed me on the spot. I don't know why – the truth is probably because I had a posh accent. But he was a nice old boy and, with time, I came to really respect him. He was committed to getting this day centre off the ground. My working life had begun.

The day centre was called New Horizon, and the plan was, primarily, to try to house people. As mentioned, we didn't have any housing of our own and so the job required us to liaise with charities that had accommodation to see if we could get people in. We had a lot of young people who, at the point at which they came to the day centre, were not up to living on their own. They tended to end up in hostels for the evening, and we would take care of them during the daytime.

Almost immediately, I recognized how utterly mountainous was the task before us. The numbers of young homeless people were absolutely terrifying, let alone homeless people in general. It was the late 1960s: a time of recession following the devaluation of the pound. For many people, life was extremely tough. The biggest issue was the simplest: not having enough money, usually through unemployment. Initially, what people needed was a roof over their head and an attentive ear to their issues. Homelessness, of course, is a perennial problem, persisting to this day. Yet, until this moment, I'd never understood what it was like. I'd never lived that sort of a life, never experienced those hardships. Besides which, running the day centre was nothing like my time in Uganda with Voluntary Service Overseas; that was highly organized. This was shambolic. We had wonderful staff, and it all worked pretty well day to day. But when something out of the ordinary happened there were no contingency plans – we simply had to try and fix the emergency as best we could.

As I got my feet under the desk, New Horizon started to accumulate people who became regular clients. One such was a young woman called Jan, a troubled person one way or another. She was a Scot aged twenty-three. She had no qualifications to interest anybody in the statutory sector, and we were the only people in the voluntary sector trying to look after her. When Jan became pregnant, we had to find somewhere to house her. After some to-ing and fro-ing, we managed to accommodate her and the newborn in an East End tower block. It was decided that she could manage on her own so long as she came to the day centre, and she was therefore supported during the day.

But this was a mistake.

One night she called me. It became immediately clear that she was drugged up and, to my horror, she revealed that she had abandoned her baby in the accommodation we had found for her. I leapt in my Mini and hurtled down to the tower block: a fairly shabby sort of place, there was no lift, and I could hear the baby crying as I was coming up the stairs. Taking them two at a time, I felt responsible. We should *never* have let her attempt to look after herself and the baby. Yet, on the other hand, we didn't have the ability to give her anything better. No local authority was interested; there was no other way of housing her. Still, hearing that baby crying out, I felt guilty.

When I burst through the door, the flat was in a bad state. There was no furniture, just a bed, which Jan and the baby both slept in. It was a mess – clothes all over the floor and everything generally unkempt. Amidst all this chaos, the baby herself was very distressed. She had been left for some time without having her nappy changed. I was still almost a child myself. I felt so helpless. I knew nothing about babies. I did not even have the experience of being around relatives who had recently had one. I struggled through changing the nappy and cleaning her up, all the time waking up to my responsibility to this child. It was horrifying. Suddenly another human life was, quite literally, in my hands.

I took her down to my Mini. Of course I didn't have a baby seat or anything of that sort, but I had managed to find a little bassinet in the flat. I popped her in that and put her in the back of the car. I sat there for a moment. 'Well,' I thought, 'what the hell do I do now?'

At a loss, I drove over to the hospital in which she'd been born: University College Hospital.

'Sorry,' I was told at the desk, 'babies only come here one way. And this isn't it.'

Explaining my situation, I asked, 'So, what do I do?'

'You'll have to go to emergency services. Either here or somewhere else.'

I took her down to the emergency facility at UCH, and they responded well. The immediate danger was over, and the baby was, for the time being, safe. But it was hardly a permanent solution. Desperate to secure her well-being, I was told by the staff: 'Sorry, this isn't one for us. It's the job of the local authority. This is for Camden.' After some wrangling they agreed to care for her for a few hours if I stayed there too. I did so until the early hours when, eventually, a social worker appeared and, finally, Camden did take the baby. But, sadly, I don't think she and Jan were reunited before Jan died of a drug overdose.

I don't know what happened to her after that. I may have been the guy who handed her in, but I had no relationship to the child. The local authority couldn't share information with me. That, as they say, was that – and with it, my introduction to trying to run a day centre for homeless young people.

But when I say, 'that was that', *that* was a truly diabolical thing.

It was to Jan and her baby that my mind turned as I stood at the foot of Grenfell Tower all those years later. I had thought about her often in the intervening years. Naturally, I had wondered where the child, now a woman, may have ended up. I hoped that she would be safe and secure in a loving family. But, inevitably, I feared that may not be the case. Either way, it was possible that she lived in a block much like Grenfell, which was very similar to the one in which we had housed her mother. As it blazed red against the summer night sky, I felt I was looking at the people I'd been working with fifty years earlier. That night they lost everything. Like Jan, they were homeless.

In the days after the fire, I began to feel this even more keenly. Oddly enough, it was more painful now than it was then. With Jan, because I was working in the context of other homeless young people, I'd got used to the fact that sometimes – often, in fact – there were no solutions. I would do whatever I could, and the care workers would do everything they could, to bring about some sort of resolution. But we knew there were no safety nets, and it wasn't easy.

At Grenfell, when I learnt that Firdaws was amongst the victims, this pain became acute. It was so excruciating because I had witnessed her brilliance. One should not discriminate in favour of brilliance, but the truth is that she really was so *spellbinding* at the event in front of Bill Gates and several hundred others. I had left feeling assured that she had a dazzling future ahead of her. She was known by her school to be a genius. It was no surprise that she was able to perform so successfully at the competition: she'd been selected to participate because at twelve she was already so exceptional.

The fact that her talent was a proven point made me feel the agony of her loss much more intensely. That this young star, of all people, had been incinerated in Grenfell with her entire family struck me as such a devastating and despicable waste. Much of the public conversation at the time passed off the victims as some sort of amorphous urban poor, but I knew only too intimately that at least one of them, and her family, were the most remarkable people. There was simply no reason for them to suffer like this. Poor Jan and her baby had the deck very profoundly stacked against them. I'm an optimist, of course, but it was clear to me that life was always going to be hard for them. On the other hand, I am convinced – as were her teachers, her peers and the inventor of Microsoft – that Firdaws had a successful and happy future ahead of her. A future that was stolen from her, and from all of us, by a local authority that should have known better.

Where the heart is

I remained involved with New Horizon for the next fifty years, becoming its chair for twenty and then, more recently, its patron. It's fair to say that the issue of where we live has always been a part of my working life, and my time with New Horizon helped to inform my career as a reporter. It's in housing that I first saw inequality writ large in British society, and it is in housing that, more recently, the excesses of inequality have proven so deadly. This chapter is about precisely that. Looking at my own experiences, both through my career in journalism and my charity work, I can only conclude that the current status quo is, to put it bluntly, intolerable.

And where do we live? When we talk about housing, so often we fail to talk about homes. What is a home?

A home is not just four walls with somewhere to rest our head. For me, as a child, home was a log fire – warmth. It was a roomy kitchen, with the smell of a Sunday roast drifting up the stairs. It was a commodious house; we were three boys. Each of us had our own space, privacy, and from our bedrooms there were lovely views through the windows. And we also had love – Mummy and Daddy lived amongst us. For me, then, a home is family, and a family is love. I think we all carry the idea of a home inside ourselves. The basics of it are uniform: shelter from the elements, warmth, a place to sleep, a place to cook, a place to wash, a place which affords enough privacy from the outside world that you might, in a quiet moment, dream.

A function of all those things combined is security. And security is the foundation on which a child builds when they go out into the world to become whoever they are supposed to be. That includes even the security to rebel. It is very hard to be daring when you take risks every day just to survive. The security that comes from having a home is the security, ultimately, to go out into the world and fail. If you have a home, you always have somewhere to return to and lick your wounds before going back out to try again.

But even before my time at New Horizon, I was beginning to suspect that such security wasn't available to everybody. At quite an early age I understood the relative apartheid which sprang from state and private education. As a child I didn't know anybody who was state-educated – not until I went to Scarborough Tech. And yet all the information we came across about education pertained to the state sector. I found that odd, even as a child. It seemed strange that my own experience of education marked me out as somehow different. It goes without saying that in the post-war period, this point of difference extended to how we were housed. The fact is, nobody I went to school with returned to a council house in the holidays.

I'm not suggesting that most children at that time suffered from abuse or neglect, and certainly not that they lived in the kind of conditions we see in many of the world's poorest countries today. But on the other hand, it's fair to say that I had no idea of just how lucky I was. I was unaware that what I took for granted was beyond the realms of imagination for many other children. For example, my mother could play piano music of any description. Mainly classical – she would play Bach, Handel, Brahms, you name it, perfectly and wonderfully. I was privileged enough to have access to my mother's talent, and the space and resources to exercise that talent; in turn, I am a lifelong lover of music. But as a child I merely thought, 'Oh, well, it's perfectly normal. There's nothing odd about the fact that you've a piano half the size of a tennis court in your living room.' Ours was an isolated existence. We didn't know that we were the exception rather than the rule.

When I began to realize that these things were not necessarily a God-given opportunity all other children could bank on, I felt extremely unhappy. I had never known that what I had was so precious. I had never known that to have your mum, your dad, married to each other, living in the same house, without violence, was a privilege. When I began working with New Horizon, I started to understand the reality of our society a little more. But, even so, it all came to me as a shock; that not every child had my sort of home life – the roaring fire, the loving mummy and daddy, the security – struck me with brutal force: it is unfair. At a deep level I understood that society shouldn't operate like this.

Though I work amongst intellectuals and grew up beside scholars, I am more of an instinctive, emotional sort of animal. Nevertheless, given the pace of events, it is often difficult to explore the wider consequences of developments. Sometimes our discussion on inequality has suffered. Too busy discussing policies and numbers in pursuit of the facts, we do not have space to explore the deeper truths. I would count class, education and opportunity as constituting a part of these truths. For instance, we may well report on a crime, and we may even cover the court case, but we are unlikely to mount a detailed investigation into the social conditions in which that crime arose. We are then unlikely to describe the conditions which await the guilty party when they arrive in prison, and what effect that has on the likelihood of their reoffending. There is rarely space on the evening news to ask why it is that our prisons are filled with more men than women, why the middle classes are less represented than the working classes, and why more than 50 per cent of prisoners self-harm whilst behind bars.[1]

A house, a home

Anybody living in a city like London, as I do, passes a homeless person every day of their lives. You may not notice them. You may not make eye contact, but they are there. If you live in any city, a portion of your community is unhoused. For me, when I ride my bicycle to work, always, every day, I pass some person who is sleeping rough. They may be sat on park benches, in bus stops, asleep on the step between shuttered shops, but these homeless are citizens of London just as much as I am. Of course, we are always in too much of a hurry to do anything – me on my bike, you, perhaps, in a car, or walking, or taking public transport. Truthfully, you couldn't do much anyway, but even the simple act of acknowledgement can sow seeds that make a difference.

We are very quick to assume that homelessness has nothing to do with us. But the homeless live in *our* society, and I don't think the scale of the problem should excuse the rest of us from pulling our weight. Even if we aren't able to do anything practical, we can at least help by donating. I think a lot of people are oblivious to how important clothes are when you're on the streets. If you've got wardrobes full of stuff that you never wear, there are people who desperately need it. The act of donating your clothes is the true meaning of society – it means all for each and each for all. Even such a small gesture helps make real this truth.

However, at a certain point, society at large, rather than the goodwill of individual citizens, must step in. I am of the view that there is a very simple solution to the problem of homelessness: we must provide homes for people who currently don't have them. This is the departure point to a wider social intervention. In a city like London homelessness is a perennial problem, but there are matters now that have made things worse: chief amongst them, in recent years, is an acute housing shortage. There are many factors driving this, but the shortage of homes provided by councils comes at the top of the list. The provision of council houses has drastically declined since the 1980s. This is true across the country, but it feels particularly so in the capital.

I think council houses are absolutely vital. For so many families, the council house has been a lifelong support. For that reason, the provision of homes should be one of the central duties of any local authority, but local authorities are finding their stock running dry. Of course, since

Mrs Thatcher's scheme allowing tenants to buy their council house, local authority homes have also provided a route to ownership. Given my support of council houses in general, it may surprise you that I'm not against the sale of council houses. I simply think that the principle established when Mrs Thatcher came up with her policy should still stand: for every one you sell, you must build a replacement. This is not what's happening. And it hasn't been happening for a long time. And both of the main political parties have failed to make it happen.

The problem of a housing shortage has accelerated not simply because the stock of council houses has been depleted. For all kinds of reasons, and I don't profess myself to be an expert, housing is increasingly used as an asset. I am, of course, a distinctly uneasy beneficiary of this racket, like anyone of my age and my income. And yes, I call it a racket, because it is. I think that if an alien came from another planet and found that the fundamental need to put a roof over somebody's head was part of some kind of deal, they'd be shocked. That an absolute human necessity is being profited from should shock all of us, but we are inured to the strangeness of it. Of course, at this point it's too late to put the genie back in the lamp, but if you're going to have a market in housing you must look after the people who cannot manage the market. So many amongst us today will never acquire a sufficient income to put themselves on the property ladder.

Getting on the ladder in and of itself shouldn't be the central issue. It's not about ownership. It's about security.

It's about achieving some equivalent of that roaring fire, of living with Mummy and Daddy, of fostering an environment where love can flourish. The human being doesn't have a bearskin, or anything else to enable us to live, as it were, in the wild. In any case, for sound economic reasons, many of us must live an urban existence. And so, for those people who have no prospect of ever earning the sort of money required to own, there must be provision. It must be stable, contractually secure and affordable. Ownership has only become so important because the private rental market does not offer these luxuries.

This issue is something that people woke up to after the Second World War, when there was a housing shortage of a different kind because of the Blitz. I remember a time when council stock was higher; indeed, by 1979, 42 per cent of Britons lived in council homes.[2] So the provision of housing is within the realms of political possibility – it has happened before and there's no reason why it can't happen again. Having said that, short of a revolution (which I don't endorse!), it's difficult to see how the principle of ensuring all people are housed will ever be retrieved. Doubtless there are readers muttering that this is pie-in-the-sky nonsense. Yet it's entirely logical that, particularly in urban areas, lower-paid workers *must* be housed. The pandemic has thrown into relief how essential emergency service workers and medical professionals are, but also that society requires people in all kinds of roles to function healthily. It's wrong, and wrong-headed, for those who work in essential roles in supermarkets, care homes or as drivers to have their income reduced still further by having to pay exorbitant rents. Without these people, wider society would not function properly. Likewise, it is wrong to force people to pay an impossible mortgage.

The current situation is not just bad for individuals caught out by the vagaries of the housing market, it's bad for the health of our society in general. In too many places in the UK, the concept of 'community' has died. The exclusive private housing that abuts the burnt-out Grenfell Tower is home to people with lives and wealth undreamt of by its erstwhile residents. Kensington and Chelsea is a fascinating example of a borough in which disparate communities are beginning to see how the wealth gap, and the failure to house people properly, is being played out. What does it do to a society when there are such profound gaps between two adjoining communities? Britain is more divided and more fractured now than at any time in my life.

To bridge the divide, today the focus is upon 'affordable' housing schemes that allow you a share, under strict conditions, in a new-build property. At the time of writing, they don't really work. You only need to look at the consequences — they have increased demand without truly stimulating supply — to see that it's obvious they are not a satisfactory solution. Any plan that must be tinkered with if it is to work — and this one has certainly been tinkered with over the years — is not a good one. I cannot believe, therefore, that the people who've devised this scheme are really looking for a wholesale solution.

So what has happened to the building plans of previous decades? After the Second World War many hundreds of thousands of houses were built, many of them council-owned. It is striking, in comparison with our own age, that in this period there was a spirit which tolerated the state doing a lot. And the state had to do a lot because we'd had a war: a lot of cities were wrecked. Government, and indeed all of us, saw it as a duty to fix things and move forward to a brighter future. Today, Britain's cities haven't been reduced to rubble by bombs, but we do live in an age of crisis – the crash of 2008, Brexit, Covid-19. After another crisis – Grenfell – I felt utterly convinced that the only solution is for the state to intervene. If you believe, as I do, that people must be housed safely, you are led inevitably to this conclusion. Personally, I think the local authority is best placed to provide housing, but central government needs to fund it.

Our culture has changed, and we're far distant from a time when the state performed this function. The difference is that, after the war, everybody was deeply affected by it. Today, due to social inequality, the elite are not affected by the problems of housing facing many Britons; they *benefit* from it. Democracy exists for just this sort of disparity. If we are to have a more equal society, we must reverse course. We must make housing a major political concern. It's happened in the past – housing provision used to be one of the hugest issues, elections were won and lost on it, and as a result a vast amount of public housing was built. Well, there isn't a war, but the crisis in housing is as bad now, if not worse, than it was then.

Safe as houses

In terms of inequality, property is the central strut that keeps the whole rotten structure standing. It is the root of all kinds of other inequalities too. For instance, the fact that two houses of equivalent size and amenities in London and Liverpool may fetch different prices by a factor of ten is a neat articulation of what the problem looks like in Britain today.

We started this book by thinking about Grenfell. The Grenfell tragedy was caused by inequality, and it left me utterly convinced that the state needed to intervene in housing. I don't think I'm alone in this feeling. What's interesting is that two very different, but nevertheless traumatic, incidents, war and fire, had the effect of requiring state involvement. The Grenfell Inquiry is forcing government to recognize many such problems. In fact this inquiry has been a model: it has been brilliant in speaking truth to the power that set it up.

The most urgent problem that the inquiry established is that Grenfell Tower was built out of killer materials. It's now been discovered that there are hundreds of other tower blocks around the country also built with similarly lethal materials. This warranted a complete change of approach. The government is now listening and there's no question that something will flow from the inquiry. In truth, I and many others thought immediately after the fire, 'Oh, this will just be a whitewash. There'll be no consequences.' But there will be consequences, without a doubt. As a journalist, I've also been interested to notice that the coverage of the inquiry is extraordinarily complete. Perhaps the media's initial sleepiness – by which I mean the fact that there was a cladding scandal waiting to be reported on, and we missed it – has meant that we aren't leaving it alone.

Nevertheless, at the time of writing there are still very large numbers of people living in dangerously cladded buildings. I reported from Salford, which suffers from having twenty-nine tower blocks clad in the same combustible material as Grenfell was. Frankly, I wouldn't want to be a minister in a government that had to deal with another tower block fire. I find it incredible that there are places in Britain where no remedial measures have been taken in the past five years. Where is the high-speed action to redeem those other cladding-blighted estates? I note that Camden Council was initially *criticized* by the public and the media for stripping its blocks of cladding within days of the Grenfell disaster. Why isn't it a point of absolute priority for the government to make sure that people are housed safely?

A central reason why is because central government is not prepared to provide funding and local authorities don't have the money to do so. The government thinks it can get away with it, which, so far, seems to be the case.

But I think that the results of the inquiry will almost certainly be so shocking that action will have to be taken. The inquiry is not a legislative body, of course, but this report will go public. Once the government is officially, and publicly, presented with evidence of the scale of the problem there will be an obligation on MPs to do something about it. And if this or any other government does nothing about it, *we* have an obligation to press the issue at the ballot box in the course of an election campaign.

I have been calling for state intervention, but of course there have been many criticisms levelled at state intervention in the housing market in the past. In the early 1990s, places like the Ordsall Estate in Salford or the Aylesbury Estate in Elephant and Castle became quite run-down. There was a lot of poverty, and a lot of crime in certain instances. The term 'sink estate' started to be thrown around, and the general perception was that the project of government playing a role in housing the citizenry had been a failure. If we are to build more houses, some of them owned by councils, what's the best defence against this criticism?

Simply put, it's no good making provision and not providing support. It's not just a question of building more accommodation – we must also enable people to live in such accommodation. We know the sorts of policies that this entails, because they are the policies that make up a robust welfare state. Our welfare state, founded under Clement Attlee, a Labour prime minister, and extended by a Conservative prime minister, Harold Macmillan, was set up to ensure that a decent standard of living was an affordable reality for all. Some of you may assume that what I am talking about here is a kind of communist treatise. But it's not. It's logical. It's reasonable, it's happened before, and it's what charities like Shelter have been talking about for years. Providing people with homes is not 'nannying', and it isn't encouraging them to become lazy freeloaders. A properly run welfare state gives people the opportunity to make a meaningful contribution to society. Ensuring a decent standing of living for all will not make the economy grind to a halt – on the contrary. That means that it's no good just building the building and shoving people in: we know this because it's a mistake that has been made too often in the past.

It's not enough to build an empty shell; you must do something to foster a community, too. At the beginning of this chapter I talked about a vision of home, and the chief thing I feel this bestows on a person is the guarantee of security. Security comes in many guises, though. It ranges from job security to safety from crime. If crime – as study[3] after countless study[4] has shown – is a by-product of poverty, inequality and a lack of opportunities, then merely making sure that the most vulnerable in our society are protected is key to fostering a safe, secure community that all of us can thrive in. Security means living in a home that isn't made of flammable materials. So, ultimately, if it's security we seek, we must ask ourselves whether we believe in a welfare state. And I strongly suspect that people *do* support a welfare state.

As for me, I don't dream of the wars and pestilence that I have reported on, but when it came to Grenfell Tower I was haunted. I woke every morning possessed by the enormity of it and of its implications. Has, I wondered, our welfare state really come to this?

Jan and Grenfell

As I stood there on 14 June 2017, watching the fire service desperately fighting the flames engulfing Grenfell, I was struck by how little had changed. Whether in the 1970s, when I was working for New Horizon, or here at Grenfell Tower, human lives were being risked by inadequate housing provision.

And yet I am an optimist. Let us not forget Firdaws. She was not from a wealthy family, but she was from a motivated family, a loving one. And they had enjoyed a degree of support from the state. Firdaws attended the local state school. She lived in Grenfell Tower, which was not, essentially, a bad place. Even though we now know it was so dangerous, it should be regarded as having been funded by all of us, and that it provided people with a place to live. For the community that lived there it was home. High-rise towers should not be villainized; they are a versatile and effective way of housing people comfortably. We must not regard Grenfell Tower as the problem – it is the inequity of the situation at Grenfell that we need to address. With that in mind, what I have been talking about in this chapter is clearly not some revolutionary idea; it is something that already exists and needs to be built upon.

I should also state clearly that I believe that people do have individual responsibility, too. Society is a blend of communal and personal responsibilities. But my worry is that the individual is being let down by the community. This is what has happened in all too many cases, with Firdaws and Grenfell as a tragic example. On the other hand, if we offer secure, stable homes to those who need them, they at least have the opportunity to exercise their personal responsibility. I like people, I think they tend to be good, and that by and large they want to take control of their lives; they only need be given the opportunity to do so. Before the fire, Firdaws' family had. She herself was the proof.

Of course, there are a few caveats. A local authority must be confident that it is supporting people who are going to use the opportunities offered, people who will go on to be self-sufficient. The expectation in providing homes is that you're enabling people to generate incomes, not that you are offering them a way out from ever doing so. There are people for whom a normal working life will prove impossible, and for such individuals a different sort of service may be required. Likewise, I sincerely hope that such a programme would lead to a reduction in homelessness. But there will always be a part of any society that is homeless because there are people who, for psychiatric or other reasons, cannot manage. We would do well to remember that such tragic cases are the tiny minority of homeless people, though. So whilst I don't think local authorities should be expected to work miracles, or that the relationship between local authorities and individuals should be one-sided, I feel strongly that we must reinvest in them so that they can provide the services they used to.

There is no getting around it: we need to build more houses. Some of those houses should be owned by the state and rented out to people below the market rate, and people should be supported so that they can turn them into homes. Yes, it is possible that if we were to suddenly start building lots of houses there would be a knock-on effect on prices: in a city like London some houses, perhaps my own, might suddenly be less expensive. But that is a price worth paying. Because we, as a society, simply must provide that fundamental necessity, shelter. Just as we, as a society, should work to ensure that something like Grenfell never happens again.

There is a question at the heart of these issues which is also at the heart of this book: what sort of society do we want to live in?

My answer is that we want a society in which there is caring within families, between families and between the state and families. With an understanding between the cared for and the carer, surely a family can sort itself out in the long run. The family must be prepared to meet the local authority halfway if the local authority is providing a portion of its income. I believe the family unit has the best chance of paying its end of the equation, and we should invest where we can expect there to be greatest return. That's not to suggest that people who have the misfortune not to be part of a family should go without support. They absolutely should be supported, as should those who, for whatever reason, choose not to get married or have children. It is more that I think family should be our starting point. As I have already written, a home is family, and a family is love.

The person who most benefits from such a partnership between state and family is the child. It is to children that we look when we wish to see the possibility of a better future. When I met Firdaws, when she spoke in front of me and Bill Gates, I glimpsed a brilliant future. And when I saw the poster declaring her missing I saw that future snatched away. If we can't, as a society, agree to invest in children like Firdaws then we're in a very bad place indeed.

I don't believe that anybody in Britain should be without a home. I don't think anybody in Britain, if they examine their feelings, thinks that homelessness is justifiable. And I don't think we're doing nearly enough about it. We did not fix our broken housing system ahead of the Grenfell tragedy. Let's take the opportunity to do so before it happens again.

CHAPTER 4

BREXIT AND BACKLASH

IT WON'T HAVE ESCAPED THE reader that I have strong views. But at the heart of my political outlook, however strong my own views may be, I maintain a staunch belief in fairness and balance. The nature of British politics means I've dealt with more Tory prime ministers than ones from any other party. As I have said, I like people, and this extends to the workplace. I may not have agreed with a given politician, and I always tried to hold them to account, but by and large I got on well with them. If I was to do my job properly, it was necessary.

But I think it will surprise people to know just how well I got on with Margaret Thatcher. I got on *incredibly well* with her. She liked pretty boys, there's no doubt about that, so I simply pretended to be one. I think most of the presenters and reporters who jousted with Thatcher found her intriguing, enjoyable and occasionally even wrong. Despite the formidable challenge that she represented in any interview, I can honestly say that I had a high regard for her. Even if I didn't like her politics, I admired her; I thought she was a courageous and effective politician. It was a very difficult time to be Britain's first female prime minister – the system wasn't plumbed for a woman to do the job – and it took a formidable spirit to take it on. Margaret Thatcher was undoubtedly a formidable spirit.

Some politicians spend their whole time looking for journalists who are on their side, and if they think you are not you don't get much of a look in. Thatcher was different. It was never difficult to get an interview with her. Her team never said, 'Come off it, she's not gonna do *you*, Snow.' That's because she didn't give a fig what your views were. The issue was only ever: will he do a good job? Will he get her to do a good interview? We had some fantastic interviews, no question. I really enjoyed the process, and I even dare to think she did too.

That accessibility is, I think, the mark of a truly great politician. It shows that you are willing to subject yourself to public scrutiny because you have confidence in the course of action that you are pursuing. So I may not have agreed with Thatcher's views, but I thought she was a top-rate politician. It was hard not to think about her during the Brexit campaign and its aftermath. There were invocations of her name on both the Remain and Leave sides. But she often emerged in my thoughts in contrast to what I was seeing, rather than by way of comparison.

Due to Brexit, we saw three Conservative prime ministers in quick succession: David Cameron, Theresa May and Boris Johnson. Thatcher was a significant politician.

You knew precisely what she believed in and you could see that, should she receive the mandate to do so, she would translate her views into a concrete reality. As she put it herself, 'In politics if you want something said, ask a man; if you want something done, ask a woman.'[1]

It has been impossible not to contrast this with Johnson. I always regarded him as a columnist: until Brexit he had been, to me, just another hack. I'm not suggesting that is a bad thing per se. I by no means think he is unintelligent, or without charm and eloquence. But he never struck me as a serious and professional politician. It seemed as if he viewed his ascent at Westminster as a game, rather than being a public servant driven by a sense of moral purpose. His support of Brexit seemed like play-acting. Even amongst his contemporaries, this wasn't the case. I don't think you could accuse Michael Gove, for example, of not being serious about Brexit: he passionately believed in it, always had.

Back in 2013, when a Johnson premiership seemed fanciful, he was, nevertheless, one of the most popular politicians in the country.[2] When the Brexit referendum was called, there was a lot of speculation from both Remain and Leave as to which side he would join. Johnson was not committed to the cause of leaving the EU before Cameron called the referendum,[3] so it was a big coup for Vote Leave when he came out in their favour. But the fact that there was any speculation or indecision in the first place seemed to confirm what I had suspected about him. Mrs Thatcher was always a woman of commitment and conviction. She was, famously, not for turning. She would never have contemplated pursuing both sides of an argument – it was simply not in her character. Once she had decided it, her view became very solid. Boris Johnson, in comparison, was a chancer; it seemed to me that he picked the side that he thought would be most beneficial for him personally.

But a chancer must be given his chance. This was gifted to him by another Tory prime minister, David Cameron. Again, when he first came on the scene, I have to say I liked Cameron. He was accessible and easy to interview. He didn't hold it against you if you asked him tough questions, and on the whole he seemed a serious and professional politician. During the coalition years, his agenda at home had been dominated by the fallout of the 2008 financial crisis; his response was to shrink the state and cut public spending. As with Thatcher, I didn't necessarily agree with him personally, but I still thought he was a good politician. He had campaigned on a platform which he was now trying to bring into reality. Nobody was unsure of what David Cameron and his Cabinet thought about public spending. Nobody thought he and, for example, George Osborne, were in two minds about cuts to the welfare state. Nobody sensed that if they faced resistance on the issue, they would immediately back-pedal. He seemed to me straightforward and serious, competent enough and willing to put himself under the microscope.

So I was shocked when he called a referendum on

Brexit. 'Whichever way this goes,' I remember thinking immediately after the announcement, 'it's going to end in tears.' It was abundantly clear that the issue would divide the country in a hugely destructive way. Worse, it was transparent to me that Cameron was using a referendum to deal with the serious divisions in his own party. A good prime minister wouldn't have needed to pursue such a radical course of action to bring his party to heel. Thatcher would never have needed to; she famously said, 'I don't mind how much my ministers talk, as long as they do what I say.'[4] There was much serious division in the Tory Party during her premiership, but she always, until the very end, led her party rather than being led by it. Cameron had gambled his tenure of power and, with it, the future course of the country. After this gambit, his seriousness to me looked superficial.

I remember the results starting to come in on the night of the referendum. From quite early on, it looked like Vote Leave would carry the day. I believed Britain was going to get poorer. I thought of my own family, my children. What kind of Britain did they face? What were the long-term impacts of this thing going to be? As the night wore on, the enormity of what had happened had personal implications for people. Jobs would be lost. Prices would rise.

Like tinnitus, a phrase rang in my mind that wouldn't be silenced: 'We've failed,' we being the media. We journalists. We had done our job poorly. We had not managed to educate the public into understanding what was at stake. I have always believed that good journalism arms people with the information they need to make decisions about how they want their lives to be run. If we tell the truth, people make up their own minds. In the case of Brexit, it was so clear that the status quo was unacceptable to people – and, yet, much of the time, the Remain camp became the public face of that status quo. In hindsight, I wish we could have highlighted more stories from those Remainers who had a positive plan for a renewed Britain, rather than focusing on the defensive and negative vision that was dubbed 'Project Fear'. In this instance, the truth weighed heavily on the positive case for a Remain outcome. The Vote Leave victory indicated that we had failed.

Let me be entirely clear. We failed not as propagandists, which we had, on occasion, been painted as. We failed as tellers of the truth. And those truths are coming home to roost even as I write. Amidst the joy of many Brexiteers, others were also asking what kind of a Britain they were going to be living in. As the night wore on, the joy of Brexiteers overwhelmed the misgivings of those who feared the consequences of their victory.

Friends and neighbours

In all the years I presented Channel 4 News, there was never an issue as divisive and brutal as Brexit. I think I can say it was the most acrimonious time for the country

I can ever remember. The Brexit campaign was a terrible episode in the history of our nation, when polarization and division ran rampant. The wounds caused by the campaign, let alone the results of the referendum, have still not healed. This chapter seeks to consider that time, to see what it tells us about journalism, government, Britain and, above all, inequality, both before and after the referendum.

I should say that Brexit posed me a personal challenge, too. In February 2016, after Cameron called the referendum, we journalists got to work investigating what it might mean. I became convinced that leaving the EU would be an economic disaster. I find it difficult to credit the idea that anybody who really examined the issue would arrive at a different conclusion.

Since the referendum, I think this conclusion has been proven to be right. The fact is, we're getting poorer, amidst weak growth and a rising cost of living. This is not solely down to leaving Europe, but it's happening, and Brexit was a catalyst. Meanwhile, most of the many benefits that were promised have failed to materialize. Inequality – which is the story behind the story – continues to grow. Add to this the costs incurred simply through fulfilling the new Brexit bureaucracy. Here is a vivid example: just yesterday, on the threshold of a documentary assignment to Greece, I had to apply for a filming visa to work there. Prior to Brexit such a thing was not necessary – I filmed there frequently without problem. To get this filming visa I had to travel to Manchester, to one of the three visa-issuing offices that serve all embassies in the UK requiring them. It should have been possible to pick it up near my home in London, but due to the massive demand currently affecting an ill-equipped system, I was forced to travel to this northern office. I spent £150 getting there and back by train, involving six hours of travel and two hours queuing for the visa officer. My total costs, and those of my crew of two, who also had to appear in person, came to a total of £1,800. An entire day was lost.

Having said this, a strong conviction is a very dangerous thing for a journalist to be in possession of. We're not supposed to have views. And whilst that's impossible, because everybody always has a view, we are certainly not allowed to share our views with the public. Throughout the campaign and afterwards, I struggled to make sure we presented the news with balance and fairness, and I was grateful for the regulatory hand that ensured this was the case. But it was an extremely difficult time for journalism, undoubtedly the most challenging of my career. Partly because I strongly disagreed with certain arguments made, and partly because certain people told lies. Finally, it was a difficult thing to report on because of its immense complexity. The case for Remain largely rested on technical legalese and bureaucratic intricacy, which, if nothing else, does not make for particularly compelling news. On the other hand, Vote Leave had a straightforward story that proved emotionally resonant: take back control. Never mind about accuracy. It was difficult to provide balance when the two sides were talk-ing at cross-purposes.

Throughout, I was becoming increasingly alarmed by the inequality story that seemed to be playing out just beneath the surface. It felt to me that the referendum on Europe was morphing into a referendum on inequality, with a stark divide between haves and have nots struck through our country. When the dust settles, if it ever does, the only good things to come from Brexit will stem from this – that it made inequality much harder to ignore. Because people had been ignored, and Brexit was a moment where they were given the opportunity to make their voices heard, they did so very loudly. We cannot allow inequality to grow so great again, because, as Brexit proves, it has the potential to make dramatic changes to our politics.

The most unfortunate aspect of all of this is that I don't feel any great confidence in Brexit leading to a reduction in inequality. If anything, the result means inequality is likely to get worse, not better.

So how did we get here?

Given where I would end up in 2016, it's ironic that I had opposed Britain's membership of what was then the Common Market. As a hack like Johnson, rather than a politician like Thatcher, my beliefs about Europe have changed over the years. I even helped Michael Foot and others in their campaign to try and prevent membership ahead of the 1975 referendum. Therefore, over the course of my life, I have held both views – Eurosceptic and Europhile. I have always been aware that the EU is, like any institution, riven by flaws, and at one time I believed those flaws were substantial enough to make our membership unattractive. But, from the point of our membership onwards, I grew increasingly convinced of the EU's value to Britain.

Besides, back in the 1970s my reluctance to join the EU was more informed by my obsession with the developing world, my experience of being in Uganda, than by my thoughts of Britain's future. I was worried about Europe consolidating a rich world in the northern hemisphere at the expense of the Global South. I could see that nations in Africa might suffer from European cohesion, because there would be more power to the European elbow at the negotiating table. Much poorer countries were desperate to export to Europe. A large bloc of powerful nations would be able to strong-arm them into unfavourable contractual terms and obligations. It's fair to say that this was a niche position at the time, but that's what guided my instincts.

My view changed between 1975 and the 2010s. For one thing, I became much more preoccupied with domestic affairs – ensuring that the country in which I and my family lived prospered. I also think the global situation shifted. From 1975 to 2010 American power expanded, and as it did I grew increasingly sceptical of Washington's leadership. Any one country's opinion, when faced with the might of American authority, was pretty ineffective. We'd always thought we had a special relationship with America, and in the Second World War that was undoubtedly true. But I felt that, in the second half of the twentieth century, our special relationship had become advantageous to America and not particularly helpful to us. It made sense to me that countries abutting each other across Europe should join in a trade and political alliance to balance out American power.

My wariness around America formed in the 1980s, when I lived and worked there as a correspondent. In Britain we had a very deep relationship with our European neighbours, and what happened in those countries mattered enormously to us, as much as it mattered to them. There was no sense, when I lived in Washington, that anyone there was remotely interested in what was happening in London. If it suited them, it suited them, but if it didn't, it didn't. My time in Washington, therefore, left me realizing how insignificant Britain had become.

It's also fair to say that when I lived in the States, I became aware of my European identity alongside my British one. America, as part of the Anglosphere, had always felt, in my imagination, culturally closer to Britain than, say, France or Germany. But you'd have to have a very robust constitution to live in America and cling to the preconceptions you had of the place before you went. It's so different to what you might imagine. For instance, in most of Western Europe certain things are just no longer considered tenable – like the death penalty. Short of a few cranks, by the mid-1980s it was a political reality across Europe that capital punishment was simply out of the question. But the death penalty was, and is, a defining element of the justice system in certain American states. It's not just the death penalty: there are all kinds of important political, cultural and philosophical points of difference. Take the issue of gun control: it exemplifies the fact that we have more in common with our European neighbours than we do with our American allies. From a distance America looks familiar, but it becomes deeply foreign once you get up close. I concluded that it was essential that Britain's future be not merely transatlantic, but continental.

As time went on, I also appreciated Europe's civilizing influence on Britain. There were all sorts of things which flowed from Europe – such as human rights – that had never surfaced in domestic British politics. I can't remember, before we joined Europe, the concept of human rights being remotely headline material at all. The European Convention on Human Rights wasn't ratified into British law until 1998 and came into effect in October 2000, so we were very late to the party. But we were much better off having got to the party, and I'm not convinced we ever would have done if we hadn't joined Europe. Human rights is a single issue amongst a great plurality. Our membership was a process of discovery, of finding out what other countries had been doing that we had not been. We learnt from them, and with time a legislative and regulatory framework came out of Europe that made things better for us in Britain.

We also learnt more about the culture of our neighbours, and I think this is so important and so overlooked. Pubs started to serve wine as well as beer. Coffee overtook tea. Our cuisine diversified, our holidays changed, so did our colleagues, our friends and our families. It's easy to forget that this change happened because it is so woven into the fabric of our life. But it *did* happen, and it was largely pretty good. Britain in the 1950s and 1960s was not better than Britain is today; I know because I can remember it. It was certainly very different, and in many ways it was worse. More buttoned up. More class-conscious. Far less choice. Many of the cultural changes that have occurred in Britain since then have taken place in the context of our membership of the EU. The source of these transformations was different to other cultural changes we've experienced, and it was, perhaps, subtler. It wasn't empire, thank God. It wasn't Commonwealth. It was neighbours. It was a continuity of land mass across which we could travel with absolutely no difficulty at all. It was the Erasmus Scheme and the Eurostar to Paris and workplaces like Channel 4 suddenly filled with expertise drawn from across a continent. Europe opened a whole new chapter for us.

Above all, though, integration with Europe brought free trade. That seems to me the essence of its benefits. Surely, we all agree that it is ridiculous to charge your neighbour to ship grain into your economy. I think that historians of the future will look back and say, 'What on earth was going on?' Free trade brings all kinds of economic benefits, that much is intuitive. But I believe it was actively wicked to pull out because of the cohesiveness that free trade brought to Europe. And look at what is already happening from the get-go: trade barriers right across Europe, with the need for permits and worse. Doing business with Europe is under threat as never before in peacetime. Did we win the Second World War to be barred from free trade with Germany and every other European country? In terms of keeping nations together and stopping them from catastrophically falling out, free trade has been one of the few things that has worked. We are used to thinking we live in a peaceful continent, but until quite recently we did not. Closer to home, peace in Northern Ireland was bolstered by our, and Ireland's, membership of the EU and the establishment of a frictionless border. Peace is always fragile, I accept that, but Belfast had significantly more of it in 2013 than in 1973. Now it is with great bitterness that I say there's a serious danger of the peace process going backwards.

Finally, on this point, the war in Ukraine (which raged as I was writing this book) looks to have been a terrific gamble on Vladimir Putin's part. Is it not reasonable to ask whether he would have been less inclined to have made such a roll of the dice had Europe appeared, from the outside, more united?

The biggest challenge of my life

At election times, Europe was not an issue that would have been raised on the doorstep when politicians went knocking to canvass for votes. If you opened a newspaper at random in 1995, you were unlikely to find headlines of haemorrhaging sovereignty, financial inefficiencies in the European Parliament or a British constitutional crisis with its roots in Brussels. Membership, when we do not revise the facts, was uncontroversial; data illustrates this clearly. Just months before the referendum, a meagre 1 per cent of the British public thought Europe was the most important issue of the day.[5] By April 2019, that figure had shot up to 59 per cent.[6] What is fascinating, though, is that in the earlier poll immigration and worries around terrorism ranked very high. In the later one terrorism had vanished, and immigration was the top concern of only 11 per cent of the population. We can infer, therefore, that Europe acted as a vector for other worries, regardless of Brexit's efficacy in dealing with them. It was a kind of Rorschach test, which resolved into whatever the viewer wanted to see.

I have often wondered whether the referendum was ever really necessary. The British people were relaxed about membership of the EU. The establishment was pro-European – meaning the vast majority of the political establishment,[7] business and finance,[8] and even some trade unions[9] were pro-European. Europe was a rare point of consensus between figures like Len McCluskey and David Cameron: they were both 'reluctant Remainers'. On the other hand, the media division was half and half. I think the BBC was objective, and I think we at Channel 4 did a good job. But there were tabloids and online resources which really went to town on leaving.

I sometimes wonder if the commitment to balance shown by broadcast media led to the unnecessary debating of non-issues in an attempt to appease a vocal minority. Prior to the Brexit campaign, an ardent wish to leave Europe was a niche position held by a fringe of activists and backbench MPs in the Tory Party. And it was the same old activists that I'd stood shoulder to shoulder with back in 1973. The generals had changed, but a lot of the foot soldiers were still in position. This, in part, was why they were successful – they had been refining their argument for forty years. David Cameron did not seem to have thought about what the positive case for Remain was.

From the outset, I felt that calling a referendum was a very dangerous thing to do. When Cameron did so, I knew there was a serious possibility that we might leave. Cameron, fresh from victorious referenda on Scotland and proportional representation, I think, did not. I could foresee how a campaign could whip people up about immigration, causing hatred and a great deal of damage. What had started as an internal disagreement in the Tory Party would draw in other actors, as is so often the case with civil war. There were obviously spokespeople on both sides who were mainstream: you could say Michael Heseltine on Remain and Michael Gove on Leave. But the referendum suddenly gave characters whose sway over the electorate had always been minimal a chance to air their views. Views that in my opinion were dangerous.

As mentioned, I regard Brexit as the most difficult issue I had to face in my whole journalistic career. You might imagine that dealing with Idi Amin, flying in his Ugandan Air Force plane and having to sit next to him was more worrying than Brexit. But in a journalistic sense the dangers back there were nothing compared to what was going on during the referendum campaign. Telling the truth in Amin's Uganda was straightforward. Amin provided us with all the evidence we needed. We simply needed to find this evidence, point a camera at it, and that would be that – it told its own story. Of course, I had an opinion of Amin's countless atrocities, and my sympathies were firmly with the victims. I defy anybody to see suffering on such a scale to respond differently. But that did not make it difficult to report the facts I uncovered objectively.

With the referendum, though, I felt anguish because my sympathies were with Remain, and I was aware that this was sticky territory. It should never happen to a journalist; one should not allow oneself to get caught up in support. But, in reality, we're human beings. I was a citizen of the country that was being asked to make a decision – like everybody else, I had to decide. This left me in an ultimate tussle between my political views and the job I had to do. All journalists knew, too, that anybody who wanted to get at us – politicians, activists and some people who might be impossible to name – was going to be well briefed. They were going to be looking for any slight indication as to what our reporting indicated about our opinions. It became a very sensitive issue. Everyone was on the lookout.

We were bombarded with mail. It was an electric topic from the get-go, and people were determined to make their point, both digitally and via the postie. Letters were underlined in red ink. I had more mail about Brexit than I ever had about any other issue and its tenor would usually be very blunt and very general: 'Report the facts, Snow. Don't get in the way of the story.' None of it was scientific or empirical. None of it zeroed in on a component of the reporting that an individual felt was inaccurate. Nobody was saying, 'Now, I've done an investigation into cost implications for the lingerie business. On April the X, you interviewed a manufacturer in Barnsley. I'm afraid that your report reached an unfair conclusion about the impact of Brexit on the import of lace.' On our side, it was extremely difficult to drill into the detail because most of the economic research suggested that Brexit would be bad for Britain. In the aftermath of the vote itself there was little evidence that counterbalanced this.

Great Britain, Brexit Britain

I'm writing about the referendum campaign from a very personal point of view, though. When it came around I was an experienced journalist inculcated with the culture, which I wholeheartedly support, that we must present both sides of an argument as fairly as we can. I have never given up on this ideal, and the referendum was not the thing to make me do so. In the end, I think we did a good job. I don't think broadcast media presented a particular bias. Besides, we have regulation in this country to ensure we don't, and I encourage this. Our work needs to be scrutinized to ensure we are doing it properly. Ultimately, journalists face this problem every day of their lives; it was just that during the referendum we had to work much harder at it.

Since the vote, Brexit has proved to be a failure on its own terms. Were we to suggest that P&O would collapse, or the pound would devalue, or that there would be twenty-three-mile road closures on the M20 around Dover, we would have had people come down on us like a ton of bricks. But the politicians knew the risks because they were looking at the same data as the rest of us. I don't think anybody who evaluated Brexit was in any doubt that it would create very serious problems.

Which raises the question: why?

Let me put this simply. I think the people who were leading the charge were probably, in the end, good old British nationalists. They wanted the Great put back into Britain. They thought that the whole business of Europe had undermined our identity and they were nostalgic for a time long gone. How to sell this to the people, though?

I didn't get out and about in the country as much as I would like to have done, but I did a good few reports of

one sort or another. Opinion differed markedly according to where you went, but I was struck by the fact that
the nationalistic seed had been so thoroughly watered.
Some would say things as straightforward as 'It's time to
make Britain great again' – mirroring the Trump slogan,
which was itself stolen from Reagan. People declared a
desire to retrieve our independence. And of course, that
one-liner of the Vote Leave campaign struck a real chord:
take back control.

Sovereignty was a massively important issue, much
talked about, but I found it a hollow excuse. We have a
unique system of sovereignty here in the United Kingdom, with our monarch as the head of state. There was
no evidence that membership of the EU had led to any
evaporation of regard for the late Queen. Affection for
the royals felt the same to me in the 2010s as it had done
in the 1970s. As for the question of whether Europe
would change our constitutional settlement or abolish
the monarchy, it was for the birds. Britain had not at all
lost its character in the years since we had been a member, we still waved flags, sang 'Rule Britannia' and
believed in Queen and Country. As far as I could see, all
of that was held intact. Our culture, like all cultures, had
simply evolved rather than remained static.

As the campaign developed, it became increasingly
clear that the danger of a single-issue referendum is that
people may not be voting on the matter in hand. In this
instance, a statement about the things they felt strongly
about could be expressed as a vote for Brexit. We have

learnt the hard way that referenda staged in democracies are an imperfect way of testing opinion. I had never worried about referenda before, or even given them much thought, because we have never much used them in Britain. On paper referenda sound absolutely fine, and purely democratic. But, having lived through a very bloody one, I think I'm now highly opposed to them; chiefly because I don't think they enable the matter in hand to be dealt with. People attach to it all sorts of other stuff which they feel aggrieved about. They are promised too much by campaigners desperate to win, and they think, 'Ah, finally, a solution to my problem.' Then, when they discover that Brexit, or whatever it might be, hasn't fixed the problem, you have a very grumpy electorate on your hands. The teachings of history are right; referenda are an unsafe way of working in a democracy.

That being the case, it was an awful time to take a litmus test of public opinion. How David Cameron couldn't foresee that austerity was going to be a big factor, I don't know. Cameron himself, and core members of his Cabinet like Osborne, represented a sort of posh Etonian, 'I'm all right, Jack' spirit – one of self-interest and individualism. But a lot of people in the country were not feeling all right. The country was going through a lot of pain. People were poorer. There had been a fall in living standards. The housing crisis was beginning to bite. Quantitative easing had accelerated money's gravitational hold on more money – wealth was becoming concentrated in ever fewer hands. The economy may have recovered, in terms of pure mathematics, but the financial crisis of 2008 hadn't ended for the average person.

Here is where the inequality component builds into this story. If 2008 had been used as an opportunity to bridge the gap between rich and poor, between the elite and everyman, things would have been very different. There would have been no need for people to fold into the Brexit referendum their more general grievances. Cameron had also significantly underestimated his adversaries; he blundered into a referendum that they had been waiting for their entire lives. They had been campaigning to leave Europe since we had joined, and now they were ready to pounce. Amongst them, a fringe within a fringe, were a group with decidedly strange ideas.

Arron Banks was born in Knutsford, Cheshire, and raised by his mother in Basingstoke, Hampshire, whilst his father managed sugar plantations in South Africa, Kenya, Somalia and Ghana.[10] His motivations for Brexit appeared to me to be centred on ethnicity and nationalism. He believed in a return to the so-called glory days of the empire – Britain sailing forth to far-flung places where we could be more, shall we say, buccaneering, rather than in ho-hum Europe where we are duty bound to follow law, rules and regulations. He struck me as a total oddball.

He was the most important thing in Nigel Farage's life, above and beyond, so it seemed to me, any cause. They were both arrogant, a similar type. I find it very difficult to encapsulate who they were because they didn't fit any known formula for people I'd come across in my working life. They were not the sort of people you ever dealt with in any other story. For one thing, it seemed to me they had an objection to Europe based purely on exceptionalism – they felt that Europeans weren't good enough to be members of our club. They seemed fuelled by an active dislike of Europe – I believe they were xenophobic, there was a mistrust of 'the other'. Although Farage was married to a German and Banks to a Russian.

Farage had a genius for saying something which was *nearly* extreme. Somehow, coming out in a plummy voice, it didn't sound so bad. He and Banks were at pains to make sure they never said anything that was actively racist, for instance. Nevertheless, there was a dark undertone to the whole thing. I always felt Farage had been dug up from somewhere, fully preserved; he didn't belong in this age. The whole dynamic of history in his and my lifetime had been about coming together – from the United Nations and the Commonwealth to comprehensive education. All of this seemed to be at variance with who he was and how he saw the world. He presented as a slightly tawdry elitist from the 1950s – right down to the pinstripe suit. I don't think there's been any other force like him in my reporting lifetime.

There was also a question over how much airtime to give them. To be clear, I would not prevent them from coming on because I thought they were dangerous. I didn't think of them as dangerous; I thought of them as absurd. Of course I was proved wrong because so many people were attracted to them, but still, they never represented anybody, they hadn't been elected by anybody. Anytime UKIP tried to enter the political fray at a level beyond the European they failed. Their presence in the Commons was minimal and predicated on defections from the Tory Party. Besides that, they didn't seem particularly keen to come on Channel 4 News anyway. Still, I didn't look forward to having to try to interview somebody like Nigel Farage. He was an unrewarding interview; he would make claims in an upper-class voice that were hard to refute in the moment if you didn't have the figures in front of you, but which, because he said it like an army officer, gave his claims authority and believability.[11] You would ask him a question, and he would say something unrelated.

A typical exchange would go like this. I put it to him, when following a line of questioning based on a figure he had used around HIV and migrants that was demonstrably false, that, 'the suspicion was that you were kind of linking HIV and immigration rather uncomfortably together'.

'No, I wasn't,' he said, forcefully.

'And perhaps a little bit of dog whistle.'

'*No*, I wasn't. What I was doing was linking [HIV to] health tourism.'[12]

I remember that Enoch Powell utilized this style a bit, too. I interviewed him only once. Like Farage, he had a very handy sneer which made you feel rather small. He spoke with a posh accent and used it to great effect to say unpalatable things. If Powell had sounded like a football hooligan you'd have said, 'That guy's a thug.' Farage never went as far with his language as Powell, but there was a mirroring in the way the British electorate responded to him – his accent masked a multitude of sins. I fear this is an upshot of inequality – the class system still breeds deference. A more equal society is not so taken in by an accent. Perhaps more importantly, I strongly doubt that a society where the gap between rich and poor had not been so brutally levered open would be receptive to Farage's message.

If Brexit was the answer, what the f*** was the question?

It was into this space that the opportunists piled in. Farage and co. blew the whistle, but what ensued from it was never as extreme as what he articulated. There was a more civilized take on what he was saying. More mainstream politicians surfed the wave of nationalist populism, and Leave carried the day.

But nothing positive, in my estimation, has come of Brexit. What good has it done us? I cannot point to a single advantage. I cannot think of a single moment when Brexit has offered us a benefit. It has so far left us weakened and emaciated and is likely to continue to do so. We are more tied up in red tape, the economy is depressed, the Northern Ireland protocol, which has brought an unprecedented period of peace, is at risk.

Brexit has upended domestic politics as we know it. The Tory capture of the so-called Red Wall was just an early part of the fallout, but, perhaps counter-intuitively, it sig-nalled a more normal turn to our politics. I don't think the subsequent elections have seen anything like the nastiness of the referendum. The Tories worked hard to make themselves electable in seats like Sedgefield, Bolsover and Don Valley. They didn't do it by using racist language, because if they had it would not have been in the tradition of the party. You can say whatever you like about the Tories, but that sort of extremism hasn't really surfaced since Powell's time – Nigel Farage could not comfortably sit as a backbench Tory MP. Perhaps one minor upshot is that the nationalist forces at work had their time in the sun, but they have nothing to hang their coat on any more.

It's this thought that makes me feel that, despite it all, Brexit has at least some potential to start putting the coun-try back together again. It has shown the political classes just how important inequality is. You cannot ignore the needs of large swathes of the electorate without them com-ing to bite you in the end. There has been, and will be, a more domestic emphasis on government, if only because of the obvious truth that ministers are no longer flying off so often for a session with the Swedes. We have suffered a traumatic and intense period, and we're still in the holding pattern. I don't yet see the beginning of another phase of British history. But, as they say, this too will pass. There will be new governments, new agreements, new ideas.

We can also learn from our mistakes. There was a fail-ure to recognize that simply being in Europe wasn't enough to persuade the population that, all in all, it was good for us. When embarking on these long projects of integration, we need to constantly nourish and renew the contract with the public. I don't think politicians did nearly enough to ensure that the economic benefits of being in the EU, which were considerable, were understood. More fundamentally, I don't think that the economic benefits were spread amongst the electorate fairly. There was a reason why the spurious figure promised to the NHS on the side of a bus resonated – people felt their public services had been cut, and they wanted more money to be invested in them. If Europe was bringing in the money, it should have been invested in public goods rather than staying in private pockets.

Whichever way we look at it, the referendum was a loud shout from the electorate that the status quo wasn't acceptable. Incoherently, perhaps, the vote to leave was democracy doing what it's set up to do: which is the people voicing an opinion on those who are in power. They were asked to channel their feelings into one issue, which was Brexit. But Brexit was about many, many other things. It was about inequality. It was about the way we are governed. And, yes, it was about immigration. There were several balls ricocheting around; we were good at spotting some, but we missed those which had the potential to cause terrible damage. They did cause that damage, and it will take a long time to put right.

I often think, if Brexit was the answer, what the f*** was the question? The referendum only asked a question about the European Union: in or out. But it became something more basic: are we happy with how things are going? The answer, evidently, was no.

If we are to reverse-engineer the Brexit answer, the question I think we should be asking is this:

'What obligation do we have to bring forth equality of opportunity? And how can that be used to guide what we do next?'

The government has the mandate from the public; it now needs to start finding the policies. But let's be candid, there is little doubt that the entire episode was a shambles and a disaster. The consequences of leaving Europe are already plain to see and it is only a matter of months since the fiasco peaked. For half a century, we have lived as Europeans sharing access right across Europe: trading freely, exchanging culture, using our political clout to bring European diplomacy forward to counterbalance Russian, American and Chinese weight in world affairs. British business and British civic society have already experienced the loss of ease in visiting mainland Europe. Diplomatically our voice in world affairs has been diminished. Many from beyond these shores are questioning how much our word and commitment can be trusted in the future. I am convinced that history will judge that the EU referendum and its consequences were a body blow to our international reliability and esteem. It is hard to find another event in British history in which our international hand was played more disastrously. As I write, it is hard indeed to imagine how our international standing and access to Europe can ever be redeemed.

CHAPTER 5

ASYMMETRIC WAR, UNEQUAL PEACE

I KNEW ALASTAIR CAMPBELL SOCIALLY a bit. Our kids went to the same ice-skating night on a Sunday in Tufnell Park, Islington. We got on perfectly well; at the skating rink things were amicable. I wouldn't say we were friends, exactly. I didn't go to his house and he never came to mine; it's not as though we'd meet up for a drink. But we had a common interest in spending an hour at the ice rink watching our children fall over.

Of course, one would shoot the odd question, but it never got you anywhere. He didn't want to talk about work and was too much a pro for a slip-up at the ice rink. But we might dissect and trisect some bits and pieces from the day's information. As soon as the gloves were back on, it was a different story. But on Sunday nights it was fun.

In those encounters, I regarded Campbell as a good guy. I knew two Alastairs: one was charming, a devoted father, a husband and all the rest of it – make no mistake, I liked him. But the professional Alastair argued the merits of going to war with Saddam Hussein. When it came to the job in hand for him, and it was a pretty nasty job, he did it very well. But I must confess that I always struggled to square the two: why did this decent-seeming guy want to do an indecent thing?

This question could have been directed at so many people involved in laying the groundwork for the invasion of Iraq. During the build-up the Government Information Services were in full swing. It was perfectly obvious that they were doing their absolute maximum to fight the cause for war on Blair's account. It was not a particularly sophisticated operation but it was sophisticatedly led, amongst others by Alistair Campbell, who knew exactly what he was doing. He was very clever at it. It led to a heated on-air exchange, despite our relationship offstage.

When we look at other wars, there is a very clear trigger. In Afghanistan, just two years before, the trigger had been the 9/11 terrorist attack; the reason to engage in warfare did not need to be sold to the people – the mechanism was clear. But Blair's government had to sell this war to the British people, and indeed to the world, because the cause was more obscure. To do so, there was a PR campaign. The tactic adopted was to bring the Saddam threat right into the British living room. It was necessary, if there was going to be Western intervention, and particularly if there was going to be British intervention, for the citizenry to be frightened of Saddam Hussein. He needed to appear as a threat to world peace.

But you had to squint to see this threat. I had been to Iraq several times. I'd seen an extremely unpleasant and menacing leader operating in a contemptuous manner towards his own people. I saw a leader who posed a threat to his neighbours, who was unpredictable and violent. But on the other hand, I'm not sure I had seen a global security threat. Saddam's ability to kill citizens in Britain seemed highly unlikely, and I therefore thought this, though it was the stated reason, an improbable cause for war. The sphere in which Saddam did pose a global threat was economic – it was the impact he might have on the oil industry, on petrol prices at the pump. But for British citizens to be persuaded that war was the right course of action there had to be a direct, personal threat. And that ended up being weapons of mass destruction and a dictator's preparedness to use them.

I can remember the real difficulty in trying to deal with this as a journalist. There were some known realities – Saddam had used chemical weapons in the past, for instance. And then there were dangers that were being credited, in some sense, to our own intelligence services. They had often done a fine job in the past, and I'm sure they would not manufacture a threat out of nothing. But it felt as though a real threat was being exaggerated to the very limit. Journalists were put in a sticky situation. If your prime minister says, 'Our intelligence services believe that Saddam Hussein could attack Britain,' it's news. You must report it. But, like many journalists with a working knowledge of the region, I was sceptical of the extent to which Saddam really did pose a threat to Britain. I wasn't an intelligence officer, of course, and not privy to the information they had at their fingertips. Nevertheless, it seemed fanciful to me that Saddam could, or indeed would, fire a chemical weapon at a British RAF base in Cyprus, and that the speed with which he could do so was a lightning-fast forty-five minutes. Having seen the creaky, despotic regime in Iraq close up, this didn't quite pass the sniff test. A threat to his own people? Yes. A threat to the region? Absolutely. But world peace? Nuclear war? These were far-flung claims.

What seemed to me to be the truth was that Saddam posed a threat to some of Britain's interests, but not the safety of its citizens.

The Labour Party has suffered from a historical problem: Winston Churchill was a Tory. Labour was always perceived to be something of a peacenik party. This is a hugely overlooked aspect of the Iraq War that I feel was the very simple core of the thing. Blair and Campbell were continuing the New Labour project of putting some backbone into the party. The invasion said, 'You can trust Labour with the security of the state.' It has a lot of appeal: we stand tall and we deal with the tyrant. I can see the appeal myself. Saddam was a brutal dictator, and Iraq, despite its oil wealth, was a shambles. Hawkish foreign policy has often played well with the electorate. Thatcher got an enormous boost from the Falklands.

Blair wanted to keep the socially advantageous

reputation of Labour – the welfare state, the NHS – but put some muscle into it. He wanted to prove to the people that Labour were as good as the Tories at defending Great Britain. Those of us born post-war do not have an active memory of war, nor of a threat to our homes. We had nothing to go by. What Blair and Campbell achieved, to some extent, was to frighten the British public into believing that it was our duty to knock Saddam on the head, and to deploy British resources in doing so. It was a domestic agenda as well as an international one.

Crucially, they weren't alone. There is no way that Britain would have engaged in this war against Saddam alone. The Americans were the force behind it, because they had a similar, but bigger, interest in the Middle East than we did. Oil. It had already been proved that a local tyrant could do a lot of damage to the world economy; the Americans obviously wanted to avoid that.

Internationally and domestically, Iraq was not viewed as a threat to Britain; it was seen as an opportunity for Labour. They could burnish their security credentials in keeping Britain safe. They could keep the Americans happy. And they could ensure the oil kept flowing freely. We misremember this moment today with the benefit of hindsight. Prior to the invasion Blair was an unbelievably popular prime minister, and with this PR campaign he managed to carry public opinion with him. In 2003, YouGov conducted twenty-one polls from March to December asking people whether they thought the decision to go to war was right or wrong. On average 54 per cent thought it was the right move. In the USA, a February 2003 poll showed that 63 per cent were in favour of sending in the troops.[1] Campbell's PR campaign was successful.

But there were large parts of the Labour movement that were not happy. I remember Robin Cook's principled and well-argued resignation speech in the House of Commons triggering a very unusual round of applause. I'm convinced that most people knew he was telling the truth; nevertheless they were all going along with it. I found myself, as a journalist, very drawn to his arguments, and I think history shows that they were probably right. Unfortunately, there were lots of cheap points to be scored: 'Oh, he's a lefty,' or 'Well, he would say that – he's a Lloyd George type. Doesn't believe in a strong defence.' Besides this, it was a very confusing time: some of the evidence we were being presented with looked like fiction, but some of it looked real. It was very difficult to determine what you were dealing with. I never felt manipulated, but I did feel that there were people trying to manipulate us.

Alongside the principled stand of a small number of politicians, London saw its largest ever protest, and there were mass demonstrations around the world. Despite this, the invasion went ahead. Saddam was toppled and then later captured. But Iraq started to fragment. A kind of civil war began, running in parallel to an insurgency against the occupying forces. The irony, of course, is that Blair ended up scuppering his credentials on security, which to some extent he had already burnished in the Balkans. Iraq showed a frustrated and enfeebled British military unable to achieve its core objectives. Although Tony Blair left office with favourable ratings overall, the Iraq War has become his legacy. He is strongly resented for it, and it diminishes the rest of us.

Does any one of us look back on the Iraq encounter with pride?

Special relationships

In the broadest possible brushstrokes, is there a starker display of inequality than warfare? Young men, often poor, are mobilized by old men, often rich, to fight and die in their interest. Moreover, in the twenty-first century, Britain has involved itself in conflicts that express a power asymmetry too. Neither Iraq nor Afghanistan were nations that had experienced the same level of economic development as Britain, and the inequality between nations is at its most extreme when they do battle. Warfare remains a tragic fact of our world, and yet its prosecution should be kept to a minimum, to the rarest and most exceptional of cases. Prior to the point when it becomes unavoidable, it seems to me that we must do everything possible to avoid it.

Does Britain do everything that it can to avoid wars? In Iraq, the answer was certainly not. This chapter focuses on Iraq whilst discussing Britain's place in the world, and international security more broadly. We need, of course, to secure our state before we can do anything else, but problems have always emerged when justifiable concerns around our safety are used as a pretext to attack others. In the case of Iraq, that is precisely what happened. Inequalities spun out as a result of the invasion, both abroad and at home, and we are dealing with the consequences to this day. In the great line of history, with events linked together by a web of causality sometimes too complex to see, one of those consequences is, as I write, the ongoing conflict in Ukraine.

To understand the invasion of Iraq, we need to understand the transatlantic partnership, and the people tasked with maintaining it in the early years of this century. Chief amongst them was Tony Blair. I don't think Blair started life as an internationalist. I don't think, when he pored over the newspapers before he became anything in politics, he raced first to the foreign section. He was an essentially domestic politician. He had an unthinking pro-American stance, and he believed that British security rested on membership of NATO – but both were easy assumptions to maintain at the time. This stance chimed with the British public, too, and it was a perfectly natural position to take. The British media was pro-American. Indeed, I was pro-American – I make no bones about it. I had been a Washington correspondent and there was a lot about America that intrigued me. But there was also a lot about America that worried me, its treatment of its own people in particular, and the absence of any kind of welfare state. Still, if you had never been to America and seen the underbelly, your view of the place remained in fine fettle.

America played a big part in my reporting career, and my personal relationship with it offers a certain mirror to our collective one. I was sent originally in 1978, as Washington correspondent. At the time, the relationship between our two countries was comradely, but I'm not convinced that Jimmy Carter was at the top of James Callaghan's agenda or vice versa. When I encountered Carter, the first US president I met, he was wearing overalls and down on his hands and knees, wielding a trowel. Carter was labouring for an afternoon on a housing project on behalf of the charity Habitat for Humanity, a group that I understand he is still working for today at the age of ninety-eight. Carter was a down-to-earth guy. He had no overweening air of self-importance, and perhaps consequently – in the larger-than-life entity that is America – he was never regarded as a great president. He is at least a great human being, as I discovered when I interviewed him for an hour onstage at London's Royal Festival Hall. Sadly, one aspect of his humanity is that he remains deeply scarred by the Iran hostage crisis, in which fifty-two US diplomats were held for 444 days by Iranian radicals. Worse, the mission he sent to rescue them came to grief when a helicopter crashed into a refuelling aircraft in the desert many miles from Tehran. I was the first journalist to reach the site some three weeks later – it was a shattering scene of crushed humanity and tangled wreckage. In a twist of fate, it was this event amongst others that led an emboldened Saddam Hussein to invade Iran, which in turn saw him use the very same chemical weapons he was accused of having the potential to use against Britain decades later.

When Reagan took over from Carter as president, many of us underestimated him. Journalists regarded him as nothing more than an actor who was a useful stooge for the Republican Party. He certainly knew how to 'strut his stuff', and was ably supported by his wife Nancy, who seemed to want him to become president even more than he did.

His campaign to unseat Carter was blessed both by the Iran crisis and by the reality that his campaign was simply more visual, more exciting, than Carter's. After the election, his panache and simplicity appealed to the electorate; he won a second term with ease. Indeed, his opponent, Walter Mondale, who had been Carter's vice-president, effectively wrote his own epitaph – 'I lost because of my inability to appear compelling on television.'

When I interviewed Reagan during his second term in the White House, we had been requested to cover the carpets with canvas, in case one of our lights exploded (as they could). Reagan came bounding in and, to our alarm, tripped over the canvas. 'God darn it!' he declared. 'You'd have thought I'd been in enough "B" Movies not to have done that!'

There were certainly those who, early on in Reagan's first run for the White House, ridiculed his Hollywood past as a qualification for the presidency. But they had ignored the fact that he had been a successful governor of California, and, in the end, even more so his balletic peace negotiations with Mikhail Gorbachev. I was struck by Reagan's charm and persistence when I reported on him, and he seemed very much in step with our then prime minister, Margaret Thatcher.

George H. W. Bush, who followed Reagan, left office with a good record and was, by and large, an effective conservative president. His premiership was marked by what went on to be known as the First Gulf War, triggered by Saddam Hussein's invasion of Kuwait. Bush quickly rounded up a coalition of nations, including the UK, France, Saudi Arabia and Egypt, and inflicted a powerful blow on Saddam, pushing him out of Kuwait. The Iraqi thorn in the American side seemed, for the time being, to have been removed.

Next was the turn of Bill Clinton, a charming interviewee. But then so was Monica Lewinsky, the young White House intern with whom, as he put, he did not have 'sexual relations'. I interviewed her exclusively for Channel 4 News in 1996 and found myself wandering Manhattan, wondering how on earth to keep the interview clean. In the end, following Lewinsky's testimony, the whole shabby parade proved to have been quite simply unpresidential on Clinton's part – he had behaved exploitatively. But it was Bill Clinton who was president when Tony Blair entered 10 Downing Street.

For Britain, Clinton was a comfortable leader. We

liked him. And he seemed to like us. Unlike many US presidents, Clinton was quite globally educated – he had been a Rhodes Scholar and studied Law at Oxford University. He was a worldly figure, cosmopolitan, and not stunted by the obsession with America that had rendered other presidents myopic. I think that was a wonderful boon for the Blair inheritance. Blair entered Downing Street secure in the knowledge that he was dealing with somebody who not only liked Britain but had been bothered to live there. That's quite a handy relationship for a British prime minister to walk into.

By contrast, when Clinton left the White House, George W. Bush appeared much more parochial. Obsessed with America, he didn't seem to know much about the rest of the world. I'm not even sure how much he knew about America. But Blair continued that transatlantic relationship with the same enthusiasm. I think he recognized that the current was flowing in the right direction, and reckoned that in strengthening this relationship, we got a good deal. Blair's focus prior to the 9/11 attacks had been domestic. Britain was going through a period of change, and there was much investment in health and education. Despite some concern at the time, I never thought that Bush was going to pollute Britain's enthusiasm and pride for our welfare state, and I don't think Blair did either. I never believed he worried that America would change our own fundamentals. The relationship worked for both parties because it provided a helpful key for the Americans to unlock the

European continent, whilst, for our part, Blair recognized that security, and our strength at the world's negotiating tables, was bolstered. Blair always had half an eye on the opinion polls at any given time, and he could see that a strong transatlantic relationship burnished his credentials as a prime minister with Britain's security interests at heart.

Underpinning all this was a shift in Britain's place in the world. It would be the last time that there was an overhanging gratitude to America from a previous conflict. The inheritance from the Second World War, and our dependence on America through the Cold War, cast a very long shadow. America drove the war in Iraq and when it decided Saddam Hussein would have to be tackled physically, there was a generation still alive in Britain who believed we owed the Americans our support. People just older than me, people who had lived through the war, people who had grown up with American airbases in our country and recognized the security America had given us for many years saw it as our duty to become involved. They may have thought the justification was rotten, but they were prepared to hold their noses. Ultimately, though, the combination of all these things left the government free to prosecute the war without any dramatic collapse in its popularity. Labour's campaign to win support for the war, to create a veil of legitimacy, was a success. They never actively misled people. They merely built upon something which was already there.

And yet, with hindsight, we can see the extent to which

Blair's calculation was off. As the war dragged on it became deeply unpopular, and even traumatizing. Most importantly, it affected the transatlantic relationship, and set us on a path to more inequality at home. It was a failure of journalism to miss this at the time. Iraq was always a distant war; it seemed to have no concrete impact domestically in the immediate term. Yet it was used to justify a doubling of the military budget between 2000 and 2008.[2] It was also an excuse to exercise our armed forces, meaning that a generation of the military was going to come through having actually seen action. All these things were pluses when it came to looking at Britain's security, but at the time we failed to report the ever-increasing stresses on the NHS. Most journalists missed the warning signs that we were heading towards the 2008 financial crisis, even as government borrowing went up to help finance the war. That's not what we were looking for: we were focused on dead soldiers, the costs of lost planes, ships and materiel, not the erosion of monies that could potentially have been spent on social welfare.

Another cost of the war that we missed at the time was the growing mistrust of politicians, and the media, amongst the electorate. As I have said, ahead of the conflict the British public were marginally in favour of the war. But there were mass protests, people on the streets in cities around the country and a huge rally in Trafalgar Square, and this rattled the cage. Campuses were ablaze with students out protesting. One shouldn't underestimate the extent of the youth opposition to it, not least because they sensed they were the ones who, if anything went wrong, would have to go fighting themselves. But the nation as a whole did not show much anxiety about our involvement.

People turned out in very large numbers against the war, but I don't think it really caused the government to think twice about getting involved. What did happen is that it modified its tone. Labour took a sober approach, removing the openly triumphalist braying that a country can be prone to during a war. There weren't endless TV broadcasts saying what a wonderful job 'our boys' were doing; there were few documentaries about hero dogs and ace pilots. The electorate was informed about what was going on, but we didn't hear much about Mr and Mrs Smith being told that their son had been killed somewhere in the Gulf, and the honour associated with their son's sacrifice. This too, I believe, had a social impact. A divide was growing between those who passionately opposed the war, those who sent people into the war, and those who had to go and fight in it. These divisions were driven by class and education; the majority of the 179 men and women who died serving Britain in Iraq until the end of the British mission in 2009 were enlisted soldiers – not officers – who are typically drawn from state schools and working-class communities. Metropolitan professionals would discuss the disaster of Iraq at a distance, but towns that saw young men return without limbs experienced it much more intimately. The crucial difference was that the former group thought the war was pointless, and therefore began to feel shame in our involvement. But the emotions in the towns of Britain were much more mixed. The war may have been seen as pointless, but there was pride in those drawn from the community who had been shipped off to fight, and a growing sense, when they came back, that they had been ignored.

When the government was discovered to have lied, is it a surprise that both groups lost faith in politicians?

The lies were made abundantly clear by the Iraq Inquiry, chaired by Sir John Chilcot. It was a hugely necessary process, but it had the strange effect of taking the steam out of the whole affair. It should shame us that the inquiry's chief findings were that the case for war was deficient, that the legal basis for war was not satisfactory, that the relationship with the USA was one-sided, and that, finally, the military action did not achieve its goals. All of these things we could intuit without having an inquiry. But what I suppose seems quite odd is that the inquiry did not lead to a huge outpouring of public outrage.

Still, it was Gordon Brown who opened that inquiry, and he suffered electorally long before the results were published – less, I think, because of Britain's military performance, more because we were so seriously involved for so long. A lot of reputations were dashed by the war, most obviously that of Blair himself. Gordon Brown became a slightly tragic figure because of Iraq. Ahead of the invasion, some of us thought Brown was so principled that he would have fought harder to prevent the conflict. It's interesting to consider what would have happened had Brown threatened to leave the government, but he never did; it may be one of the things which weakened his reputation as a prime minister. Brown had a lot of fans, of whom I was one, I admit. But he did not emerge from the war strengthened. He looked somehow reduced – yet another politician who went along with it. Of course, we may say that he had inherited a bad hand, but he played it terribly by doing so little to resist the war. Had he put his head above the parapet, it would have been shot off. Still, that would have been the course, suicidal though it was, of a truly principled politician; as I have mentioned, it was Robin Cook's course. I suspect Brown thought he could get more done in power than out, and I can understand the logic. He was a good man faced with an absolutely impossible choice.

I admired Gordon Brown. By this time, inequality had become my personal focus. Brown had long battled it. He was clearly devoted to a modern welfare state, and I thought he was a very articulate exponent of its value. I think his principles as a man were right. I did not know him well personally, but what little that I had seen of him socially, I liked. He was a voice for a positive kind of politics. The war, undoubtedly, was very damaging to those issues. I do not like to think in counterfactual terms, but it's clear to me that a Brown premiership without the war

in Iraq smouldering in the background would have had
a different focus. Brown's aim, and really the stated function of New Labour, was the eradication of poverty,
particularly child poverty. This was clearly at odds with
a war fought for corporate interests.

With the benefit of hindsight, the greatest tragedy of
the Iraq War is that it achieved the opposite of what it
sought. It was a fight on behalf of the corporations and
big businesses that, today, actively harm our security and
society. It is entirely clear that the greatest threat now is
climate change. But the Iraq War was fought so that we
might continue our abuse of the atmosphere by bolster-
ing the companies at the sharp end of the petrochemical
business. We use more energy than ever before, and we
urgently need to transition to a source of energy that is
not carbon-based. It's interesting to think that if the Iraq
War, and our involvement in it, had never happened, it's
very possible that we would have woken up to what is
happening to the environment two decades earlier. At
the time, petrol at the pump was becoming increasingly
expensive, and the hope was to reduce the burden on
consumers, keep the cars on the road, the planes in the
sky and the money flowing around the economy. But
today this looks unbelievably short-sighted. I'm not sure
enough people have recognized that the Iraq War set us
back years in the fight against climate change. Shoring
up the flow of oil around the world by virtue of a military
operation kept us from beginning the hard, but very
necessary, work of transitioning our energy supply. It

was a war rooted in our absolute determination to hang on to petrol.

As I said, I don't like counterfactuals as a rule, but I can't help but consider a different way in which problems concerning our energy supply might have been resolved in the early part of this century. The anxiety around gas being cut off could have persuaded us to go for a new alternative. The pointless investment in the war could have been routed to the momentously important investment in new energy technologies. Britain and the USA could have set a course to ensure that subsequent generations would enjoy clean, safe and abundant energy, created in our own nations rather than bought from dictators. But it didn't happen. And now it's happening too late.

Energy for war, war for energy

That story continues to this day. The current war in Ukraine is not ostensibly being fought over oil, unlike Iraq, but disrupted energy supplies and attendant price rises are a knock-on effect. European dependency on Russian fossil fuels has emboldened Vladimir Putin, leaving him feeling both financially and militarily invulnerable. Had the West seen the writing on the wall for fossil fuels before the war in Iraq, we would be far better prepared for the situation we currently face. Ultimately, British interests will be weakened as we go into a period of great economic uncertainty.

Still, the conflict in Ukraine has deep roots and, just as Iraq shifted the balance of power globally, the war in Ukraine is very likely to do the same. Russo-Western relationships have been fraught for my entire life, but I think we have entered an entirely new era. Before, it was very easy to have an Iron Curtain. It's only today that we're paying for it. Nothing was achieved in the Iron Curtain era beyond ensuring that the Russians never came in and we never had to go out, as it were, to deal with them.

Today, there are many striking points of difference. Most obvious is the lack of mass Russian support for bad behaviour. We're not seeing demonstrations of support in Red Square. Of course there are parades, and there is much chatter through the Kremlin's propaganda outlets, but these pale in comparison to the groundswell of support we would have expected to see as a matter of course in the past. In previous eras, at the very least, millions of people would have been marched out to fill Red Square with adulation for their great leader. Well, the great leader is not looking so great. He is also coy with the Russian people, refusing to clearly state that the nation is at war, even as the number of Russian soldiers returning in body bags is mounting in the tens of thousands.

Russians are becoming increasingly aware that their nation is not looking like the force it was. Ukraine's resistance has been remarkable. It has turned history upside down to some extent. It is an extraordinary moment because it's beginning to make us look at the past and wonder, could we have done things differently? When I went to Russia, even in the Gorbachev era, you realized the place was absolutely decades behind us. People's way of life was very hard. There were long shopping queues, with citizens wrapped up in layers because the heating was largely non-existent. It was a backward state, one you couldn't come away from saying, 'Hey, that's the future.' You simply couldn't – it was the past.

Still, for most of the twentieth century there was a presumed genuine threat that Russia could invade Europe, and that by extension it could end up being the pre-eminent power in the world. That was something people worried about; I worried about it very much. I grew up convinced of it. My parents told me about the Russian menace. I remember feeling the extraordinary embarrassment when Yuri Gagarin journeyed into outer space. The Russians had beaten us, and were ahead of us. But I look back now and ask, was that an aberration? How did such a dysfunctional place perform such a scientifically astonishing mission?

If the war in Ukraine has taught us anything, it's that, without nuclear armaments, were there to be a confrontation between NATO and Russia, Russia would lose. Even in this significantly smaller confrontation in Ukraine, it's a real class act to lose your primary warship – the biggest warship in the fleet, the most modern, sunk in a matter of hours by a Ukrainian missile. That's an unbelievable military failure in a war against what is, undoubtedly, a lesser power. Despite failures in Iraq and

Afghanistan, the American military never suffered anything like such a catastrophic loss. From a Russian perspective, Ukraine is not a France, or a Germany, and it's not part of any major alliance that protects it. It's not part of NATO or the EU. It's a singular country bound up in the history of the Soviet Union. Many people have discussed the Ukraine War in the context of history repeating itself, but in many respects it feels like the inverse of the Cold War.

There is a historical resonance, however: it is with our war in Iraq. Just as in Iraq, a war of aggression has been started which may prove humiliating and damaging to its prosecutors. A year before the war, I suspect 'Ukrainian Nazis' were just about as live an issue for the Russian people as were Saddam Hussein's weapons of mass destruction for the people of Britain. And just as in Iraq, dishonesty is at the heart of the affair. In the past century, Russia has been, supposedly at least, a paragon of equality and opportunity. Putin himself has confessed his sympathies for a socialistic world view and claims to keep his membership card of the Communist Party.[3] Yet the immediate consequence of events in Ukraine is that we can identify some of the richest people on earth, living in some of the most expensive houses ever known to humankind, complete with vast wodges of finance sitting here in Britain, and they are atop the Russian tree. These are the people with whom power resides in Russia; they are a financial aristocracy – the oligarchs. The upshot is that, by certain measures, Russia is the most unequal society on the planet, with its richest 10 per cent owning 87 per cent of the nation's wealth (by comparison, in the UK the richest 10 per cent own 44 per cent of the wealth).[4] Just as the war in Iraq diverted attention and resources away from public goods, so too will the war in Ukraine. The difference is that, after decades of corruption and mismanagement, Russia is significantly poorer and more unequal than Britain.

Vladimir Putin is, of course, no communist, whatever he claims his sympathies are. He presides over a broken nation. He is, according to some estimates, the richest man on the planet.[5] He also has the aura of someone deeply unpleasant – neatly encapsulated by the twenty-foot table required for the foreign minister to brief him from the far end. I've never met him properly, but I have been in his presence. His face was fixed in a cold, piercing expression and I never once saw him smile. Beyond that, the proof of the pudding is in what we've all seen. Most striking of all is the sinister business of sitting at one end of that extremely long table whilst apparently conducting negotiations. You cannot seriously be trying to work with someone when you plonk them at the far end of a massive table and sit at the other end. The symbolism is absurd. It has been suggested that this preference was influenced by the still-unfolding coronavirus pandemic but, come on, Putin, you're not so beautiful that you couldn't wear a mask.

I see in this physical divide – at one end of the table possibly the world's richest man, and at the other the international community – the divide which is at the heart of this book. Russia provides a cautionary tale. It has become a winner-takes-all society. There's an enormous division between the haves and the have nots. And the haves won't even extend a decent arm to try and pull up the have nots. When we allow politics and society to become oligarchical we lose control, and the interests of a tiny minority end up masquerading as the interests of all of us. Having such wealth at one end of the spectrum skews our politics, causing terrible decisions to be made, often at the expense of the average person. It's clear that corporate interests in the USA ahead of the Iraq War had the president's ear more frequently than those who had less access to money and resources. Yet, for all our sakes, listening to the needs of people – on jobs, security, economic growth and, above all else, an environment in which we can live and breathe – would have led us down a very different path. It's far too early to say what will happen between Russia and Ukraine. Still, with the political problems associated with securing fossil fuels high on all agendas yet again, I can't think of a better time to start investing in a supply of energy that is purely our own and has the additional benefit of not destroying the planet.

Wars almost never work out the way in which their principal architects expect; Blair certainly could not have wished the Iraq War to turn out the way it did. War is, by nature and definition, volatile. We must secure the state. But the most reliable way to do so is by establishing and nurturing peace.

After the battle

As the Iraq War blundered on, my children grew older and the skating sessions began to dry up. I don't think it is because of Iraq that I stopped seeing Alastair Campbell. Nevertheless, our relationship had become a little bit bumpy and there was a certain amount of avoidance. It was cool for a time. I think that these days, should our paths cross, it would be as friends.

As the Iraq War recedes from memory, I feel in the end that it marks our loss of something as a nation. We have become a client state when it comes to deciding who we're going to fight with – meaning that we are subordinate to the USA and serve its interests. And we have become a client state when it comes to handling the wealth of those we should be least disposed to. We lose our dignity in both instances, and dignity is a hard thing to regain. What did the invasion of Iraq do for us? It perhaps taught us the hard lesson, learnt seemingly once a generation, that wars of aggression invariably do more harm than good. Post-Iraq, we seem to be living in a more conflictual time. Brexit was not a military confrontation, but it was a period of struggle for Britain. Despite all the conflict, we're becoming a diminishingly important state. We haven't got the influence that we had through being in the EU. Nobody is interested in small countries bellyaching about the fate of the world, and we have little to back it up with when our military is shown to be beholden to our alliances. I fear that it is in precisely such dysfunctional times that governments make the spurious assumption that the solution to their problems lies in a foreign adventure. I'd wager that's at least in part what has happened with Mr Putin. But if we wish to secure peace, we are often better off looking inwards rather than outwards.

For instance, one extremely unfortunate upshot of the Iraq War was the growth of home-grown Islamic extremism. The 7/7 bombings, the bombing at the Manchester Arena, the stabbing of Lee Rigby – these acts of terrorism flowed inexorably from our wars in the Middle East. We had never experienced a Muslim born in a British city taking up arms against his fellow citizens before this. Thankfully, terrorism remained a very minority interest for our sizeable Muslim population, which itself speaks of our cohesiveness. At the same time, the far right and their fellow travellers succeeded in stirring up anti-Islamic sentiment. Yet we are nowhere near either group's apocalyptic vision of, and desire for, all-out conflict. This isn't to diminish the terrible atrocities committed; it is merely to say that following the Iraq War both Islamic extremists and the far right tried to divide us, tried to show that our multicultural society is dysfunctional. But it's not. We're a remarkable multicultural society. Truly remarkable. And we should treasure and nurture that. It's an irony, then, that the only existential threat Iraq ended up posing to us was when our own social fabric started to fray as a result of the war.

Despite attempts to disrupt the course of our own

society, the current still flows in the opposite direction. Kids of all races and religions are still successfully educated together. This speaks of a British dignity which in some other areas has been dented. Of course, there are examples of cultural separation, but I think we're amazingly integrated, all things considered. I suspect that the average Briton does not pay much attention to the various ethnicities of the people that they inevitably encounter over the course of a day. When I consider the intractable divisions and segregations that I have seen between different ethnic groups in other societies, I feel proud of ours. We should never take our cohesiveness for granted, nor think that it is a finished project; but we have a flourishing multicultural society whose watchword remains tolerance.

If we are tolerant, by and large, domestically, why is it that we seem incapable of being so internationally? There were those who said, after the weapons of mass destruction turned out to be a red herring, that Saddam was a dictator who had to be removed because the fact of Iraq's difference was intolerable to the international community. He was part of what was then termed an axis of evil. But actually, in our communities at home and in the international community, we regularly tolerate massive differences. We are allied to Saudi Arabia despite its many profound contrasts to our own way of life. We may have differences with others, but it doesn't behove anybody to get involved in violence in a misguided attempt to level them. Tolerance is a low threshold to clear. It is not the same as acceptance or love. But we would do well to cultivate this old-fashioned, common-sense value in our international affairs as well as our domestic ones.

When it comes to levelling differences, internationally and domestically, there is a much more effective solution than bombs and guns. We need to strike at the root of the problem – inequality. A more equal, democratic world is far less prone to conflict. Our misguided blunders in the Middle East, and Vladimir Putin's so-called special oper- ation as I write, should serve to underscore this point twice in red ink.

PART TWO

THE NEWS

CHAPTER 6

THE NEWS TALKS BACK

A NORMAL MORNING BACK IN the early 1980s, and I'm a reporter for ITN. The alarm goes off at 7 a.m. and, as I drag myself out of bed, I turn on BBC Radio 4, which I'll listen to unrelentingly until I leave the house. My antennae are sensitive to anything new. Anything that's changed. It's odd, perhaps, that I should turn straight to the BBC because my own radio experience was in the commercial sector with LBC. But I regard the BBC as the most trusted and dependable news source. Its sheer spread of correspondents around the world means it's more likely to be right than most.

As I cook and consume my porridge, I'm picking up any developments on stories we had been reporting the day before. These may well come during the *Today* programme, in which there are key interviews with relevant people. If something entirely new has happened, it will be the first glance I get of the shape of the day. As I'm listening, I'm always trying to fathom what the editors are going to get me doing. There will be a home editor, a foreign editor and then the big boss editor. Whilst I'm having breakfast they are already consulting each other, starting the wheels turning ahead of the day's formal start. But for me at this stage, unless something truly major happened during the night, I probably haven't been contacted by the office; I regularly go into work without having had a conversation with anybody. Whilst listening to the radio I enjoy the morning's guesswork. It often happens that, as the day unfolds, I'm surprised by what I end up working on – it is one of the pleasures of the job.

Breakfast done, it's time to grab my bike and head over to the office. The bicycle is the secret aid to good journalism. This was true in Washington, Rome and Moscow, and it's certainly true in London, too. It sounds ridiculous, but the bicycle is a fantastic asset because you can guarantee how long it will take you to get from A to B. That's a hugely important thing to be able to do in news. You've got to know what your parameters are, otherwise you may miss the moment when you should be supplying the office with the material they want. There is also very little that can prevent you from completing a journey that is begun on a bicycle. In a vehicle, a bomb crater in the road, a police roadblock or, in London, the humble traffic jam can stop you in your tracks. But a bicycle is nimble. You can dodge the bomb crater, skirt the roadblock and swerve between the stationary cars.

There are many places I have loved riding my bike as a reporter, but undoubtedly my ultimate favourite ride was to the ITN studios at Gray's Inn Road in London

WC1. Which, on this normal morning back in the early 1980s, is precisely where I'm heading. As I pedal, I'm ruminating on what the day has in store. These twenty daily minutes are a great moment for thinking. You have not got any passengers; you have not got a driver. Nobody's going to interfere with your thoughts, except for the occasional bus that cuts you up or a bit of angry horn-honking. It's a daily ritual where I order my thoughts. You may experience a similar kind of calm in a cab or on the Tube, but I, unfortunately, am now unable to jump in a cab without the driver saying, 'Here, aren't you off the telly?', or a Tube carriage without somebody earnestly asking, 'Mr Snow, tell me, what did you think about what the prime minister said last night?' When cycling from the office to an event, to an interview, to an incident, I find myself ruminating quite constructively about how I'm going to handle it, what I'm going to do, but also where I'm going to lock the bike up. There is a hard-core peloton of journalists who ride a bike. I don't know who they are, but I am aware of them whenever I get to the heart of the story, only to find myself in a battle for who gets the lamp post.

I get into the office by 9, ahead of the 9.30 editorial meeting. I make a beeline for the editor. Between breakfast and bike, I was following a ghastly new development in the Eastern Bloc: the Russians have assaulted one of the states they'd rather have more hold over than they do currently. I want to be in on that story. I want to get it. So I grab the editor by the elbow ahead of the meeting and say, 'Look, I think I can get you the Russian ambassador, he might just give us an interview. We go way back, and I'm sure I can get him at short notice over this thing.' I have known Russian ambassadors in the past, but it's possibly the case that I'm doing a bit of bragging and exaggerating too. Perhaps, in this instance, going way back means 'doing an interview once five years ago', but that counts as a foot in the door.

TV journalism is competitive. I'm in competition with the other hacks in the building, but, of course, we are all in competition with the BBC and whoever else. I'm wagering that the Russia situation may well be the lead story on the evening news, and I want to be a part of it. To do this, I must contribute something. There must be something new in the story for it to become 'news'; I'm hoping my interview with the ambassador will be just that.

Clearly, there is a lot of ego in play, and I would say I have a vast one. I hope I seem at least somewhat down to earth in general, because that's part of the sales pitch. Journalism is a competitive, cut-and-thrust environment, and you won't survive without a certain degree of self-assurance. But it's competitive and it's also co-operative. There's a strange balance between egocentric individualism and teamwork. There may be colleagues who really do know a lot about this breaking story, and going in with them will ensure you can make it a win for the programme. So, having spoken to the editor, I may grab a colleague or two for a quiet word ahead of the meeting – it's important to get one's ducks in a row.

Despite its importance, the editorial meeting is quite casual. We're usually sitting around on sofas. There's no placement or explicit hierarchy; it's not as if you always sit in the same place. The editor's role is to introduce the big new story and draw out what people may or may not know. It could be that there is somebody who has a handle on it, but they might be modest in coming forward, or they might be keeping what they know to themselves for reasons of competition. It's the editor's job to ease them out by saying, 'Come on, Doris, you know this. You were only just in Russia. Tell us what you know.' There is something quite familial about it; nearly every member brings something to the table, and like a family, sometimes there are disagreements. But in general it is a very fertile team.

The editorial meeting is when we set the day's agenda and figure out how we're going to handle it. For example, if a story will still be developing when we are on air, we may need to have a live element from the scene. On the other hand, perhaps it's just as effective to do it all from the studio. Will we have the footage we need by the time we go on air? Will it be finished? Will there be a transmissible story by the end of the day, or would it still be in action? It's quite stressful, because you never entirely know whether something is going to come off for you. But it's adrenalized and exciting, too.

Having made my pitch for the day, I'm told who my crew will be – the camera person, the sound person. Usually it's just the three of you; normally the reporter is his or her own producer, unless the story is so big that it requires somebody doing that job full-time. If a story demands other bits of input that the team on the ground can't actually get hold of, you'll have a producer to pull these parts in. The producer also takes charge of the shoot. There's usually some nice to-ing and fro-ing between the reporter and the producer as to how things should be done.

Having a bit of, if not conflict, then at least diversity – of opinion, of perspective – is an essential component in keeping everything running smoothly. It often means that you don't miss things. It's incredibly useful to have another pair of eyes on the whole business. Of course, there are many eyes, not just other reporters; there are services like Reuters and the Press Association (now PA Media) which dribble out information all the time. They are already inputting to the story we are trying to make, too. The truth is that no news organization – no radio station, television channel or newspaper – can do all the work. Signing up to agencies such as Reuters or the Press Association allows a lot of material to be gathered from elsewhere. In our Russia story, perhaps there has been a strong reaction to brutality in Eastern Europe in Beirut – protests that have turned into riots – in which case we might turn to Reuters or one of the American networks to get local input on that angle. Back then, this would come through ticker-tape machines; there would be printed paper pouring out of a machine with information on it. The newswire doesn't give you everything, but it might help you discover the names of key people involved in what was happening. It's then up to you to make an effort to contact them.

When it comes to contacts, the first port of call is your own contacts books. Do you already have the number of the person you need to speak to? Sometimes you surprise yourself: 'Good Lord, how do I have *his* number?' The contacts book is a priceless item. A journalist is as good, or as bad, as their contacts. I have perhaps three or four books, and they're ratty. Scruffy. Every single page is filled with cards, with several updates, new telephone numbers, new locations and all the other little bits you scrawl in: *Former ambassador to Cyprus. West Ham fan.*

If the person you're after isn't in your contacts book, he or she might be in somebody else's. If you're at base, you'll call out in the newsroom: 'Anybody got so and so's number?' After that you might try a few friends in the business. You might ring a politician, or somebody in the civil service, and you might even be able to get something from the secretary or somebody who has even the most tangential connection. There are endless ways to find somebody when you want to do so badly enough. But it all comes down to the humble telephone, tied to the wall on your desk.

This sometimes makes that post-editorial-meeting moment a little delicate. A group of journalists are rushing around a big open-plan office space, jumping on the phones and trying to get a lead. You can never be sure whether the mood in the office will be competitive or co-operative. This may mean that whilst I'm on the phone I'm covering my mouth so that my colleagues don't know exactly whom I'm speaking to, or what about. More importantly, my contact book is closed. Some contacts are so valuable that it's better to try and keep them to yourself. You don't want somebody scrawling down your Russian ambassador's phone number whilst your back is turned.

After an hour on the phones, and a quick bite, I have managed to wrangle a meeting. I've been given a producer because it's a big story. I have my camera operator and my sound person. We're off to the embassy. But, invariably, because my team have equipment to carry and I don't, I go by bicycle and they take a cab. That means that they get stuck in traffic whilst I have a bit more time to play with. As I'm cycling across town, I have a light-bulb moment: 'Of course! My old pal John Smith, he'll know something about this – he has a feast of a contacts book! I'll ask him!' A quick phone call was not an easy thing to make. Back in those days, you were very dependent on phone boxes, and what accompanied the existence of a phone box was vandalism. Rare was the day that the first phone box you encountered was operational.

Thankfully you find one that isn't in bits, and thankfully John Smith is at his desk. 'The guy's a complete arse. Cold as ice, doesn't care a damn for journalists. He'd much prefer to be back in his old job than giving briefings to the likes of you. He's a very hard man to get through to. Still, if he does agree to talk to you, whatever you do, *don't* mention Afghanistan. He'll clam up entirely. He made a huge cock-up on that front, and that's why he's ended up in London.'

Good to know.

I find the embassy and, even with the pause for a call, I probably have an extra fifteen minutes before my team arrive. Prior to leaving the office, I stuffed a whole wodge of cuttings from News Information in my pocket. I start reading through them. Newspaper cuttings, photographs, photocopies of pages from books, all from the library at work. I'm rummaging through to find any other interesting little details that might assist my interview. News Information was one of the most important offices in the building; because everything was paper and tactile, and therefore damageable, the guy there would often insist on retrieving the material himself and then passing it to you, very delicately, to ensure it didn't get torn and wrecked for the next consumer. It would be photocopied and shoved in my pocket for just such a spare moment.

All of this has informed my thinking on what I want to ask in my allotted slot. By the time the team turn up, I've scrawled down some illegible questions in my notepad. The producer and I have a quick exchange of thoughts. A secretary comes out: we're on. The ambassador will see us, but he can only give us five minutes, rather than the ten we'd been promised. We complain, but that's that. Five minutes.

In the interview, I'm trying to drive the conversation

to the essence of the story; I'm trying to get him to actually *say* something about the matter. I know that, by and large, the answers I receive will be a variation on the theme of 'Well, I don't know anything about that, I'm sorry to say. I think you may have come here under some kind of an illusion.' Or alternatively he'll start mentioning things that I can't get my head around. There's a sudden reference to something that happened in Iceland. My mind races – 'Heavens, well what on earth was that? Cod wars. No. Natural disaster? Who knows?' It may be something that you can only resolve when you get back to the office and are able to go through the cuttings again, to see whether you can make sense of what he said to you. It may simply be distraction.

I think I am a reasonable interviewer. The best interviewers are the best listeners, and I may not be the very best listener. However, without over-flattering myself, I think I have an ability to try to charm my interviewee into some degree of indiscretion. I think in effect you're trying to persuade the interviewee that you're on his side. You're not there to take his trousers down and whack him on the bottom. You're there as a friend, as somebody who will be helpful to him during this difficult time. You might shuffle through a variety of roles very quickly, trying to find the one that will get him to talk to you. It may even be 'By the way, Ambassador, what did you make of *West Side Story?*' Anything, literally anything, that you can find that will put him at his ease, make him feel comfortable, before you get on to the things he will find uncomfortable. It's a very odd human activity. It's two people trying to work out who the other one is. And it all happens very fast.

'Mr Snow, I think you've had enough time with the ambassador now.' The gatekeeper is here to move you out before you make anything like a personal connection. I like sometimes to try one over the shoulder. 'So, Ambassador, if I say that the Russian forces did use slightly excessive force, that'd be OK with you, would it?' The over-the-shoulder remark often provokes a response. Disruption is the begetter of information. They think you're on one side, and you suddenly say something surprising, which suggests you are, in fact, on the other side. Such an approach can get them roaring at you to get out, which, of course, says a lot more than 'No comment.' But the important thing to remember is that our ambassador need not say anything at all, just so long as the cameras catch the moment. An expression on his face can tell us all we need to know. That expression could be that thing that we were looking for all day: news.

Still, now that we've got it, what do we do with it? Time is the most important thing. If it's 4 p.m. something else may yet happen to affect the story. If it's thirty minutes to transmission, beyond tinkering with your script, there may not be much you can do to reflect whatever just developed. The team race back to Gray's Inn Road and straight into the edit suite. The editorial process is near-constant; we re-edit anything that we've done to reflect whatever we've managed to pick up in the course of the last few hours. The process is physical. We are just entering the videotape age, and that means we have to chop and stitch footage together to create our broadcast. Still, this is better than the waning film age that preceded it – back then we had to develop the footage, which took at least an hour. We are living through a period of immense technological change. The new medium is inflexible and it's hard to change things last-minute, which runs the risk of the story being out of date by the time it broadcasts, but it still buys us a lot of time. There used to be quite a bit of frustration because you might have learnt something which you hadn't been able to weave into your report. There'd be nothing you could do about it.

We've made a story. It's got footage pulled in from different sources, and the crown jewel is the interview with the ambassador. We have him looking horrified as I ask a question over my shoulder. The team are feeling pretty good about it and, to boot, the editor comes in to say that this is the number-one story of the day. The programme starts to air at 7 and we're all still in the building. We watch as the show unfolds live, and there's a mixture of reactions – some people, fatigued, smoke to keep their eyes open, some people are itching to get to the pub, some are alert and attentive. In just a few years' time, I will become anchor and I'll be there reading the news, but at this point I'm just a reporter.

When the show is over there's a debrief with the editors and possibly, though we don't crow about things too much, a few patted backs. This being the early 1980s, plenty of people are off to the pub, but to my immense good fortune I had viral hepatitis early on in my career and I can't stomach much alcohol. I cycle home. It's 10 p.m., meaning there's time enough to watch *Newsnight*. Then, bed by 11.30 sharp, as I need to be ready to get up the next day and do it all again.

The changing face of news

This second part of the book will look in more detail at my life in journalism, and the challenges journalism faces in the future. I believe that journalism is vital in fighting inequality. But journalism faces its own set of inequalities, too, along with a whole host of other problems. In terms of inequalities, journalism is not an easy field to enter, and there's a risk that the disparities in society get transmitted into the newsroom. When that happens, important stories about race, class and gender could be missed. Ultimately, if journalists are all the same, they are going to have blind spots and overlook stories. As I said, even back in the 1980s, having competition, different voices and a range of experiences and ideas helped the team produce a better piece of journalism. That feels true now more than ever.

I retold a day in my life as a reporter at ITN in the early 1980s to show you both how much has changed and how much has stayed the same. In many ways, a journalist's day looks very much the same in 2023. Today I wake up and it's Radio 4 and porridge, just as it was back then. But it is also the BBC homepage on my phone. It's the newsletters and reports that I subscribe to from the major newspapers and magazines, along with my own emails and my social network. Anything I pick up that's interesting I'll try and chase by going to one of the wires, now online rather than spewing paper all over the office, or simply by googling. Emails, texts and calls are pinging back and forth between me and my colleagues from the moment I wake up – making my cycle into work all the more essential these days. It's one of the rare moments when I can clear my head.

When we arrive at the office, we are armed with significantly more information than we used to be. And when we are briefed on who is going where, and with what team, the possibilities are greater too. Whereas previously getting a camera across London and filming was unwieldy but possible, we can now move the whole programme to Paris, or Kyiv, or Washington should we need to. The camera held by a camera person is much smaller, and much of the basics of an editorial suite can be taken with us in a laptop. We don't have to develop film or splice pieces of video together. The digital revolution has affected every part of the recording process – from obtaining footage to projecting it into viewers' houses. And I would say it's been a positive development.

I still maintain my contact books, but I can just as easily track somebody down via LinkedIn, or a few Google searches. I'm constantly asking around for a bit of background on a subject, but I haven't stepped into a vandalized phone booth since I first got a mobile phone. News Information was disbanded in the 1990s, and I don't cycle around London with newspaper clippings spilling out of my pockets. I still might try the old over-the-shoulder remark, but these days it's as likely to be caught by a passer-by on their iPhone as it is by my own crew.

That passer-by effect is new. Whilst barriers to enter the newsroom, to my chagrin, do exist, the barrier to becoming a journalist has been considerably opened up thanks to new technology, not least the mobile phone. You have a far more sophisticated piece of broadcasting equipment in your pocket than a team of three could carry around in the early 1980s. We live in a filmed world. Our reports may contain footage from dashboard cams in cars, or grainy mobile phone footage, or a GoPro strapped to a soldier's assault rifle. This has brought a new challenge – verification. Previously, we could verify our footage because we made it ourselves, or it came from a reputable news agency. These days we may receive images of a supposed military victory through social media, but it can be very difficult to prove that what is being claimed is actually what happened. We may see a picture of a battleship being blown up in the Black Sea, but we must interrogate these pictures to make sure. We'll ask experts to check and double-check. We'll see if there are other videos like it. We'll seek eyewitness accounts. What we won't do is simply throw the pictures on air. That, on the other hand, is an option open to the would-be citizen journalist: you can post whatever you like on social media.

I mentioned being in competition with newspapers and the radio back in the early 1980s. There is much talk today about broadcast news being in competition with social media. I'm not sure it's quite the same thing. In general, images and information on the social network demand verification. Social media has barged in on those agencies we used to rely on, throws pictures at us, but we have to start from zero in trying to verify what they really are. We have to, in short, do the job of a journalist. For that reason I feel very comfortable about the future of journalism, because, in a sense, social media has proven that you can't have pictures without human interpretation. When you do, you run too high a risk that the viewer will end up misinformed. My only fear is that we stop worrying about people being misinformed.

Everything has changed, then. And nothing has. I still end my day watching *Newsnight*, even if now I also scroll through people's reaction to the show on Twitter at the same time.

It may sound boring to do the same thing the same way for so long. But the truth is I still find the news invigorating. You're always learning something new, wrestling with a different argument, challenging yourself. And, as I have said, I have a big ego and journalism is one of the areas where such an ego can be soothed. The process is the same, but the technology has changed the kind of outcomes we might have, and the technology itself has always been changing. What it didn't do is change *why* we did our jobs. Nor should social media.

I believe in journalism. I believe it can make a difference. I believe, in fact, that it is the best tool that we have against the inequalities I lined up in the first half of this book, and in this section I'll make my case for why.

Why good journalism matters in the digital age

We live in a factual world. It matters that people are educated and aware. Technology may have changed, but we must still strive for the same standard of truth that I was persuaded to pursue when I started fifty years ago. I think the danger of allowing phoney facts to become a major element of human existence is very dangerous indeed; it will lead to actions and activities and tensions that have the potential to threaten the kind of world we live in. Not getting your facts straight causes genuine conflict, ultimately even war. Unfortunately, I fear that we are being asked to consider the possibility of living in a subjective world rather than an objective one. We can't, not without the risk of major conflict. Journalism matters because if you can establish the facts between a broad group of people, between individuals and society, they have the potential to understand each other.

But it is increasingly difficult to have that broad consensus of what the facts are, and, as we see, it seems increasingly as though people don't understand each other. It doesn't surprise me that during this period of enormous change, people have become more polarized. Now that's not to say that I think there's one group of people – journalists, say – who have a stranglehold on facts. The more people who are involved in the pursuit of truth, the better we all will be for it; and transmitting the truth is fundamental to a functioning and modern society. In an age where there were no planes, no cars and no flights it perhaps didn't matter as much. But now that we are, in terms of both communication and information, so much more connected, the truth is more important than at any time, in any age.

I am hugely optimistic about social media, the internet and the pursuit of truth in the long term. But I think we are passing through a difficult, adolescent stage with technology, and we need to make certain decisions. We have got ourselves into a place currently where social media platforms prioritize emotions over objective reality – emotions like anger or outrage, for instance. For the time being, that's a problem. But I think that these emotions, in the fullness of time, will prompt people to seek out the truth. That may be biased reasoning, because I'm a journalist and I believe that people want to know the truth, but there you go. I've no evidence to support this, but my hope is that there is a natural instinct in humans to say, 'Really? Is that true?' Of course, as journalists we go to a second and a third and a fourth source to confirm something, and the average person doesn't have the time or inclination for that. But they want to know that the information that they are receiving is true. Indeed, my hope is that, with time, respected news outlets will serve as verifiers for the things that people may see on social media. They already do, to some extent.

Despite my optimism, it would be foolish to blind ourselves to the risks of social media organizations – risks that, in a sense, look like a repetition of some of the things we've seen in the first half of this book. ITN in the 1980s was independently regulated. Twitter, in 2023, is not. Last year, Elon Musk, the billionaire car manufacturer, bought it. Like it or not, Twitter is a news source for a lot of people. Indeed, I used to tweet a lot when I was a full-time journalist because it was one way to report on a new development. There's a lot of very good journalism on Twitter, well put together, well thought through, ably verified and justified. I have been amazed by the growth of so-called open-source intelligence, and of the citizen journalist.

But equally, Twitter is more open to manipulation than, say, Channel 4 News or the BBC – not least because it isn't staffed by professionally trained journalists. There's plenty of stuff that's just plain inaccurate through no kind of agenda, and plenty of stuff that is plainly inaccurate through the very obvious agenda of a state or a private citizen. If Twitter were owned by a private person, and that person had an agenda, there is an enormous risk that it will be used to promote such an agenda. I think the general perception is that Elon Musk is a clever fellow, and I don't have a specific problem with him, or really anybody else, for that matter. My problem is that I don't think there's any human being on earth who should be unleashed with that sort of power. The issue is not simply about *who* owns the thing, it's about the ability to own it in the first place. Owning what has been described as 'the public square' is a wholly new and previously unimaginable kind of power, and it brings a wholly new and previously unimaginable kind of inequality.

The first answer that pops into anybody's head is regulation. But who, in this instance, regulates the regulator? Social media is qualitatively different to broadcast news, which I think benefits from regulation. The news I've historically been involved in flows from a single jurisdiction, and the regulation is overseen by a democratic process. I'm at peace with this. Where would we begin to start regulating social media? At an international level? From the UN? Or here, in Britain? Truthfully, I don't know. It's a very difficult question because there is a genuine risk that regulation would destroy social media, and the trouble is, like most people, I enjoy its bracing freedom. I've enjoyed being on it and using it. I've benefited from being able to use it, and I think our news reporting has benefited too. I have 1.4 million followers on Twitter; that's more than the nightly broadcast receives.

If journalism is the key to fighting inequality, then I believe it will have to find a way to rub along with social media. Social media has the potential to make journalism, and even the world, better. The trouble is, it has the potential to make journalism, and even the world, worse too. Our country feels more divided in this social media age; it needs bringing together as never before. Part of the capacity to do it, we have in our own hands. We must reach out, connect and empower. Social media is a space that seems to allow for this and, certainly, this is one of journalism's chief functions. Yet we seem more disconnected and disempowered than ever.

There is another, growing problem with the relationship between social media and traditional news organizations. The digital media companies must pay more to display other people's journalism. At Channel 4 News, short videos we produce can spread through Facebook like wildfire. They are accurate, fact-checked, verified and balanced, and people obviously like them because they share them with their peers through the network on a monumental scale. It cannot be beyond the bounds of human understanding to come up with a way of ensuring that these mega-entities pay news organizations fairly for providing this kind of content – which, after all, helps keep their customers happy.

Facebook, as things stand, both facilitates and threatens broadcast media because of un-fact-checked information. Yet whilst its uptake by the young is beginning to fade, I cannot deny that it has been brilliant in enabling us to reach new viewers, to innovate and to get attention for some of the world's most important news items. Facebook feasts on our products and pays all but nothing for them. This cannot last. I'm a fan of Facebook, but I'm not a fan of playing fast and loose with the products that we in television news generate at great expense. Naturally we embrace and revel in the digital age. But we cannot let the massive power of its barons devour our sources of information for free.

Still, this isn't even the greatest problem. A significantly worse one is the fact that proper journalism is hard to monetize online because it turns out that fiction is stranger than fact after all. Certainly, it's more compelling. Our reports may be spreading like wildfire, but that doesn't mean much if a fabrication is burning through the internet like napalm. The same algorithm that privileged our report can just as easily showcase fake news, and on an unprecedented scale. We must, as a matter of absolute urgency, change this and prioritize veracity over virality. For instance, we could have some kind of independent ratings service, much as we do for financial institutions, that allows us to see the creditworthiness of different news sources. There is a dystopic possibility if we don't: we will end up in a vicious cycle – with ever more extreme and partisan sources of information reinforcing people's prejudices and causing ever more vitriolic news feeds. This is a world where accurate news, eventually, dies out.

Private news and public goods

Given that profit is at the heart of this problem, we cannot understate the importance of having public-service journalism in this new media landscape. You only have to look at market forces to see the undeniable public demand for such broadcasting. If you add up all the BBC's output – iPlayer, website, World Service, TV, radio – the total reach for it, and by extension the total demand for it, is titanic.

I believe in public-service broadcasting. I think it offers a distinct and different, but responsible and trustworthy, provision. I am glad of commercial equivalents, but they don't have the emotional hold over me that the BBC does. I find discussing it an experiential thing. I have grown up and lived in a world in which public-service broadcasting has been a reassuring guide that has never let me down. Its very existence is a kind of regulatory force. The BBC is something with which people in the commercial sector must compete. That's healthy. It raises everyone's game. It's just like being at ITN in the early 1980s – competition between colleagues, including those journalistic colleagues working for other outlets, brings out the best in us. My hope is that the same will prove to be true of social media. It will push everybody else to do their jobs better. We can already see something like this happening. The BBC has responded to the desires of a generation who cannot remember a time before the internet. The BBC's website, iPlayer and BBC Sounds are all ways in which younger people engage with the BBC without ever using its core televisual offering. Other broadcasters have had to adapt. It has the potential to be a virtuous circle, one I would prefer to see us in rather than the dystopic scenario sketched above, where we compete to tell the biggest, strongest, most clickable lies.

There is a crucial role for public-service broadcasting, then, just as there is for social media when it comes to driving down inequality. If people are well informed, they'll be able to make better decisions about their lives. If the news media don't have a public element to them, you run more of a risk that they'll lose their ability to fight inequality. If all those organizations, online, in print or on our screens, are owned by private interests, who serves the public good? A private interest will, on some level, have an agenda; even if that agenda is as simple as being profitable, it still creates the potential to skew the informational landscape. At the very least, public-service broadcasting provides an alternative.

And providing an alternative is crucial. As I have said, journalists don't have a monopoly on truth; we need to readjust as new facts emerge. Equally, we may be subject to assumptions based on misinformation, just like the public. It has happened to me in my own reporting life.

When I first went to Iran, the only reporting that I'd seen from the place was American. But, over very many visits to the country, I came to realize that there was a dif-ference between the Iran I encountered and that which the US media had established. The American account depicted a country which was godfather to numerous terrorist activities, was backward, and irrationally reli-gious. The reality I discovered, with which America seemed unable to engage, was that this was a very sophisticated country with an educated population, whose way of life was being significantly undermined by the way in which powerful agencies – all of them in private hands, of course – tried to portray it.

The reality, the truth, was much more complicated than the story that was being told. Despite the strenuous efforts made to undermine it by both the US press and Iran's own theocratic government, there was a notable capacity in the Iranian people for creativity. For art, for critical thinking, for survival. I had arrived in Iran assuming that its people would be inescapably foreign to me, that I would be unable to recognize them, or that we would have no common ground. This wasn't the case at all. I tried to show that in my reporting, and I hope it made people reassess their own assumptions.

Journalism, for all its faults, is an absolutely cardinal element in our understanding of each other. There are many efforts made around the world to distort and disrupt, and there always have been. Journalism pushes back against this. It has the power to say, 'No, actually, I think you'll find it's more like this.' That is a force for good globally. The world would be a very much poorer place if that ability to say 'no' were systematically extinguished, whether by profit, disinterest or the agenda of those who would try to own the news.

CHAPTER 7

PRESS FREEDOM

Advocating for Iran

IF I'M EVER ASKED WHICH countries I actively enjoy
working in, I reply that one of them is Iran. I can't dis-
guise the fact that I relish the place as a country and a
culture. My first experience of Iran was gained having
arrived overland from London. It was one heck of a journey. I was headed for India. Some twenty universities
were brought together by an ambitious stunt called
Comex – the Commonwealth Expedition to India. There
were twenty-five students on each of the twenty buses,
and effectively we drove in convoy all the way from Cal-
ais to New Delhi. But for me, this stop, in what once had
been Persia, was the most intoxicating, despite the absence
of alcohol. I was young at the time, just twenty-one years
old, and a student at Liverpool. Surprisingly perhaps,
other than my time in Uganda, it was my first trip abroad.

I was immediately struck by Iran's sophistication and
splendour. It's so noticeable when you arrive in Iran overland; you realize what an exceptional place it is within its

region. There is a kind of imperial glory to its architecture, typified by fabulous mosques and public buildings. The arts generally – poetry, literature, music especially – matched the buildings. There was a sense that many people were highly educated and culturally aware, and fluent communicators of their civilization's contribution to history. Of the many places that I've been all around the world, Iran stands out to me as one of the most beautiful and culturally rich. This is counterbalanced these days with recent history – tension, war, the constant clash with America. It was during my reporting there that the Shah fled and the Islamic Revolution of 1979 took hold, an event that had worldwide repercussions.

When I arrived there on my way to India, Iran was still under the Shah. It was a very unequal country, and in that sense it did not appeal to me at all. But I was immediately taken by the people. Iranians had a very clear understanding of what their problems were and of the value that Iran brought to the world. When I travelled there again to report on the Iranian Revolution, I witnessed the dynamic of the place change dramatically with the theocratic state it ushered in. The Shah was, to some extent, a kind of Western creature. He'd been captured by the West in economic terms, but he hadn't managed to carry many of his people with him outside of Tehran. Still, even after the revolution, during the many times I returned, the people I met remained fantastically welcoming and very easy to communicate with. All in all, it wasn't a difficult place to be in or to report from, unlike other theocracies such as Saudi Arabia. I became convinced that Europe and Iran, and even America and Iran, were much closer in certain important ways than I had been led to believe by what I thought I knew of the place.

I would return to cafés where I had been before as a student, where we had sung pop songs and there were now Revolutionary Guards carrying pistols. People no longer attempted to engage us in conversation, let alone sing the Beatles with us. There was a much greater preponderance of the unmistakable Mullahs, with their head windings and dark cloaks. But there was still, too, the whiff of a reminder of the beauty of the place and of the people themselves.

I visited Iran extensively as a reporter. The overwhelming issue over the course of my relationship with the place has been the Islamic Revolution, which was ferocious. I use that word not speaking exclusively of the violence, though there was violence, but also regarding the absolute conviction that faith was the be-all and end-all for the country. Yet despite the apparent clampdown on Western pop, and though there is still much more to Iran than simply Islam, these days Islam is a profound driver of its culture. The revolution, therefore, somewhat flattened those other aspects of Iran. It also eroded people's freedoms. It was very absolute in its administration – it was hard to see a country I loved going down a path I didn't feel suited it in every way.

It became more and more difficult to report from

there. The administration was wary of journalists. But I had good contacts from previous visits and a high degree of access. Beyond that, the Iranian people remained educated and retained the memory of freer times. I recall such intimate details as sitting on a kerbstone talking to people, quite casually, despite the fact that an Iranian talking to a Westerner represented a suspicious development for the law enforcers. People were brave if they were talking to us. They did so because they were driven by a higher purpose. They wanted the world to understand what their problem was with the Iranian Revolution. It was not so much the loss of the Shah, I don't think many people minded that at all. It was the loss of Iran's place in the international community that vexed many Iranians I spoke to. They wished the outside world would continue relating to them; the average Iranian wanted to be part of it. As I said, this was a sophisticated, cosmopolitan country, and its middle classes mourned the loss of that outward-looking sensibility. It may have had very underdeveloped areas, but Iran's greatest asset was its dynamic and brilliant population. It was a depressing sight to see them suddenly so constrained by the absolute embrace of Shia Islam.

Press freedom, certainly as I conceive of it, wasn't a concept that the authorities in Iran saw as compatible with their theocratic beliefs. Prior to the revolution, I knew many Iranian journalists. A good number of them were arrested and served long periods of time in jail. I could reach them with the occasional bland letter, read ahead of schedule by the authorities, whilst they served their sentences. But it was very difficult to get a sense of how bad their lives had become, and thereby do them the service of reporting on their condition. Yet even in a theocracy the media is important. It's my belief that, in a state like Iran, press freedom is not a threat but an opportunity for the authorities.

If the Revolutionaries had not been so paranoid, they would have a much better time of it both in Iran and internationally. Iran was not going to be a nation where the many educated people would readily and easily give up on freedoms they had previously enjoyed. A dialogue involving the press and the people might have resulted in a situation in which certain echelons of the citizenry were more understanding of what the Mullahs wanted to achieve. Unfortunately, this dialogue never happened. Repression became the norm and, with time, more extreme. In the same period, the image of Iran that was reaching the West was inevitably one of tyranny. There were ugly developments, ranging from the death sentence to incarceration, and horrific scenes of police brutality. The world looked on aghast. Iran's reputation became toxic. And economic sanctions followed.

Iran is, I think, a very good example of a country where oppressing the press, and eroding press freedom, actually damaged the place very considerably, not just the people but the regime too. If the regime had sought popular approval, if it had opened itself up to criticism, and by extension tried to persuade rather than demand, it may

have been more effective. The Shah was a very unpopular character. Only the elite got anything out of him and
he was, by and large, dreadful for the country. The Mullahs could have got a good number of people on their side
if they'd understood this and played it rather more effectively. Instead, they simply became their own elite. And they
still are. By any test, they are a relatively long-surviving
revolutionary entity. Yet the fascinating thing about Iran
is that the people themselves have never really changed.
They remain intelligent, open and, in many instances,
harshly critical of their leaders. People who want to talk
to us have found ways to make it work, despite the enormous risk.

The revolution happened a long time ago now, though.
As the generations pass, those with clear memories of
how much freedom there was are dying off. In time, Iran
runs the risk of losing its ability to speak freely, because
free speech is not simply a legal framework, it is a habit.
So much will be lost if that comes to pass. The lack of a
free press disgraces a place internationally, but more
importantly it diminishes it internally, too. To have such
a vivid and brilliant tradition of literature and art replaced
by the sterility we see under the Revolutionary Guards
starkly underlines this.

The deepest shame, and the most perplexing misstep
from my point of view, is that Iranians are the greatest
advocates for Iran. Were Iran to have a free press, there is
no doubt in my mind that its people would not be merely
criticizing the regime, they would be celebrating and

advancing their culture, too. The message many people around the world receive about Iran is unremittingly grim and negative, and at odds with my many experiences of the place. Give Iranians a megaphone and I believe that they will tell a story that the world will want to hear. A free press, then, is not simply a check on power; it can be a successful power's greatest asset.

The press wasn't free under the Shah, but, in contrast to the revolutionary regime, it was significantly better. Losing a relatively free press was not an act that protected the place, or helped develop it, or even brought about greater fidelity to the regime. It was nothing more than a grotesque and monumental act of self-harm. This was horribly advertised in the British context through the utter suffering of Nazanin Zaghari-Ratcliffe, recently returned, finally, after six unimaginable years of incarceration.

The tools for equality

As I've written, journalism is one of the best tools that we have in order to fight for a more equal society. But journalism cannot exist unless a state and its citizenry are prepared to maintain a free press. There is a constructive tension between the state and the media. In the best cases, one feeds the other, the jabs and nudges that journalists give to politicians encourage them to improve, and the politicians provide the journalists with rich material to report on. But if politicians see journalism as a thorn to be removed, rather than a spur, there are always disastrous consequences.

This chapter makes the case for a free press. It shows why the ability to criticize leads us inexorably to a more equal, better-functioning society. A free press gives people a voice, and that is the primary thing a citizen needs when advocating for themselves. But these freedoms are relatively new innovations and they are not necessarily the norm around the world. A free press is also not static – freedom must be maintained. The world of news has always been unstable and press freedoms are often under attack. Freedom waxes and wanes in all countries all the time – including Great Britain.

A free press is also something that we perhaps don't think about much of the time. It seems theoretical or even philosophical. Let me be clear: it isn't. It's an intensely practical issue which defines a country, enabling it to understand itself and present itself to its own people. It is a country's greatest international advocate, and the main device by which it learns and improves. Given that I feel inequality is so often driven by decisions made in ignorance, this educational process is essential in creating a fairer society. Just as in Iran, when you shut down a free press, you do not simply stop a country from criticizing itself, you also deny it the freedom to celebrate itself. Of course, in places without a free press we see displays and pageantry, military parades and flag-waving. But this is hollow. It doesn't lead to the same creativity and innovation, to growth or improvement. A free press doesn't necessarily mean that everything that is written is true, and it doesn't necessarily ensure good journalism. No press is perfect. But what is certain is that oppression always results in a worse outcome.

Shining a light

When we look at a truly disordered state, it is usually very hard to find a free press in any meaningful sense of the word. In my career, one of the most difficult places to report from was Uganda. As you know, I had visited the place prior to becoming a journalist, thanks to having done Voluntary Service Overseas. But during the long years of Amin's dictatorship it became almost impossible to report from there. In fact, it wasn't worth it – it became dangerous for journalists, with hostages being taken and reporters attacked. Eventually, reporting became so tricky that the international journalistic community largely stopped going. It ceased to be a country that you investigated because you could not function properly.

This was a crying shame. If you highlight a country like Uganda, it has the potential to become a live issue for the international community, and therefore perhaps lead to more aid, and indeed trade. Sanctions could be placed on unjust leaders. Without a free press, or indeed, in Uganda's case, any kind of press, it is impossible to turn the spotlight on injustice, removing even the ghost of a chance of doing anything about it. This cuts both ways. As mentioned, an even greater difficulty is that there's no natural kind of process for praising what is good, because repression becomes the only story. To return briefly to Iran, I sense most people are not aware that every Iranian child enjoys some sort of education into adolescence and beyond. That's a success story, and it's one that is not true of other theocratic regimes. But without a free press, we kill off any dispassionate attempts to evaluate a country or its merits.

A free press is unusual in much of the world. The world's ascendent economy, and perhaps its latest superpower, does not have one. Surely, you might be forgiven for thinking, China operates perfectly well without a free press. But I'm not so sure. Firstly, I fear that China is unable, in the West at least, to tell its own story, and that has a bearing on its relationship with nations like America and bodies such as the EU. More generally, despite the Chinese economic miracle, cracks are starting to form in the façade. Successive waves of the Covid-19 pandemic have proven a monumental problem for China. Despite pursuing a 'Zero Covid' strategy, millions and millions and millions of people have caught it, many of them becoming gravely ill, and yet the degree to which the Chinese government has reached out to other countries to learn how they have coped is small. That a nation will do nothing to alleviate the suffering of its own people if it means, potentially, losing face is clear evidence that it doesn't have its priorities straight. China's disconnect from the rest of the world has been writ large throughout the Covid crisis.

Unfortunately, we, along with the Chinese people, do

not know the real scale of the problem, nor how long it has been going on for. We see markers of the effect of China's 'Zero Covid' policy in the economy, but we don't see, not clearly at least, the real toll of the virus on the population. An intriguing component of this is that, for a long time, particularly in the early days of the pandemic, here in the United Kingdom many people looked jealously at China. There were mutterings to the effect of, 'Well, you know, maybe it's not great to live in an autocracy in certain ways. And maybe I don't personally approve of some of the things that they have been doing. But they got a grip on Covid-19, didn't they?' As it turns out, they did not have a grip on Covid. They had a grip on information about the crisis, to the detriment of all of us.

In the very earliest days, if there had been freer-flowing information in and out of China, it is possible that the world's reaction to Covid-19 in those crucial first months would have been different. We'll never know if that would have changed the outcome, and, as I have written in a previous chapter, I'm not one for a counterfactual. Nevertheless, a free press in China would have played a positive role in finding a solution and in determining how best to protect the population. If you have a free press, you have a dialogue. You can debate things. In China today there's no debate. The state decrees, and this has created terrible suffering, some of it needless.

Right at the beginning of the pandemic, Dr Li Wenliang warned of a dangerous new virus infecting patients in his hospital in Wuhan. He was investigated by the police and told to stop spreading rumours. Still, were it not for Dr Wenliang's bravery, we would have learnt about the presence of this virus – which was, even at that point, freely circulating around the world – weeks or months later. This news just about managed to sneak out under the censor's nose. Can we imagine what would have happened if it was amplified by the full force of local and international news media? Covid-19 has proven that clamming up, trying to prevent people from knowing the truth, doesn't work. It may look as if it does for a time but, in the round, the consequences are disastrous. To restrict information, particularly in the time of a pandemic, is foolhardy.

Covid-19 was an interesting test case for a free press in the West, too. It has worked as an informant on the importance of a free flow of information. The British government, for example, was open about what it did and did not know about Covid. Those daily press conferences were a mechanism for the government to talk to the population and tell them what it thought they should do. We in the news media aired contrasting views, with individual epidemiologists advancing different evidence and ideas and putting them into the public realm so others could interrogate those ideas. There were many epidemiologists who said that a lockdown was not a good idea, and that we should allow the virus to circulate. On the other hand we had other epidemiologists saying, 'I think we need to lock down significantly harder than we actually are.' A free press allowed these different scientific views to be aired, and enabled the public to engage in the debate around their own fate. Just think: three years ago, the average person had not the faintest clue what an epidemiologist did, or what an R-number might be, or how a virus could be transmitted via aerosol. It was the free press that educated the population rapidly, to the point where the average citizen held an informed view on matters of extreme importance to their health.

Covid-19 was also an experimental moment because it showed what happens when free presses interact with repressive regimes. I think the best way of protecting journalists, and indeed making the cultural and political case for a free press, is to engage, not to cut off. We must use our engagement to talk openly about things that are wrong. Now, of course, that may result in you having your ambassador sent home. But, perhaps surprisingly, it doesn't happen that often, and if it does, the principle still stands. It is very interesting that sometimes there's enough information getting into these repressive regimes to make a difference and bring about some sort of change of attitude.

Covid-19 came during a period of change in the attitude that we in the West have to gathering news, too. When it comes to world issues, the age of posting teams and correspondents across the globe is all but gone. To get to the root of what is happening, we have to invest in and trust local freelance reporters. Using local people on the ground has the potential to make the news more reliable, as a local will always have greater understanding and access than somebody parachuted in from London for a couple of months. The sheer cost of sending our own people to live and report in many countries that are persistently in the news has become prohibitive. The news coming out of China in the early days of the pandemic was being spread by local Chinese doctors and journalists, often at enormous personal cost. The war in Syria is a similar case in point. The dangers for a foreign correspondent have simply become too deadly, and the ability to gain access is nearly impossible. Hence my editors employed Waad Al-Kateab, a Syrian freelance journalist and film-maker – remarkable, multiple-award-winning and recently Oscar-nominated. Waad made a series of harrowing films for Channel 4 News simply titled *Inside Aleppo*, which exposed the horrors of the largely ignored Syrian conflict. Her husband was a doctor in one of Aleppo's last surviving hospitals; Waad, still in her mid-twenties, was self-taught and we added to her training – she had amazing access, and created important work that would have been impossible otherwise.

The Syrian War is one of the most photographed, recorded and streamed in human history. And yet rarely since the Second World War have the parties involved proceeded with such obvious impunity. Madaya was a town with a Wi-Fi connection but no food. Hence the outside world saw every bomb that hit this small place. Every bomb that hit Aleppo, too, was broadcast online. This is all the more remarkable because Syria does not operate anything like a free press. The regime under Assad is psychopathically and murderously repressive. For somebody to report as candidly and openly as Waad has done for Channel 4 News shows extraordinary courage. One of the really inspiring things about her is that she's a mother as well as a reporter. She's had two children in the course of her career; one was with her in Aleppo throughout the whole siege. I wonder if it acts as a kind of armour. *For Sama* – the name of her own young daughter – brought the brutality of war all too vividly to our attention. I remember a particular moment: a young mother carries the corpse of her son, Mohammad – he'd been shot by the enemy. Waad had lowered her camera, but the mother and others near her called out 'Keep filming.' 'I understood at once,' Waad told me later, 'the mother wanted the world to witness her anguish as her murdered child lay in her arms.'

Whilst I don't know whether Syrians themselves are aware of Waad's reportage, I believe that Syrians, like all people everywhere, understand the importance and power of having their story told. This can only happen in a world where information is able to flow freely, where journalists and the press are not seen as enemies but as servants of the truth. Yet being a journalist is dangerous. As I write, one of the many tragedies of the war in Ukraine is the number of journalists, foreign and local, who have been attacked by Russian forces. Any journalist or editor looking at Ukraine right now must see that if the country is overrun, the danger to those individuals who so courageously report it to us in the West is acute. The camera provides a two-way street. It shines a light on an injustice, but it exposes the reporter too. The Russians have recordings of what journalists have written and spoken, and they'd spare no effort in going after these people, either locking them up for ever or worse. This problematic duality of the camera is perhaps insoluble. But it means that when we in the West receive reports from places in the world that don't enjoy our freedoms, we have a responsibility to understand the risks people have taken to cause information to flow to us, and we must honour them by, if nothing else, looking and listening unflinchingly.

A free press in Britain

Moving from this very insecure world to a more stable one, we in Britain nevertheless have challenges to press freedoms. They're different, obviously, and they're not equivalent; but in giving the full-throated defence of the free press that I hope this chapter represents, we would do well to look at ourselves in the mirror. A cornerstone of the free press in Britain has been the BBC – the rules under which it operates mean that the freedom of the press is legally mandated and baked into its constitution. But the BBC is under threat.

There is a strange belief in the Conservative Party that private enterprise is the answer to all needs. This is a positively religious conviction in certain quarters, and it defies all logic. There is no sector in which faith in the private sector is placed more readily, and more ignorantly, than the media. Such people will point to the fact that there are numerous extremely profitable and successful media operations which are private companies, not state-owned. Then there's the BBC.

I have never worked for the BBC, and I therefore feel at complete liberty to express my unbiased thoughts on it. Let me be totally clear: both as a journalist and as a citizen, I've depended upon the BBC my entire life. It is, inarguably, the greatest public-service broadcaster in the world. I truly admire its achievements, and I think the average person, and certainly the critical politician, is unaware of the fact that, in the media sector, the BBC is the envy of journalists the world over. There is no question on that point. If you go to America, or France, or Nigeria, or Japan, or really *anywhere*, objective, first-class journalists in your destination country have only good things to say about the BBC. Is there a greater mark of approval than the admiration of your competitors?

I'm a considerable consumer of the BBC – of its radio, televisual and internet-based provision. As a consumer, I have a message to politicians: you touch it at your peril. I don't think any government would dare come forward with a campaign to privatize the BBC, but we run the risk of death by a thousand little cuts. This is utter madness. Funnily enough, the philosophy of current Conservative free marketeers is that competition is a good thing. I wholeheartedly agree. Placing a public-service broadcaster amongst private ones makes for a more comprehensive type of competition in the marketplace. I think that the BBC, Channel 4, Sky News and others all prove very useful as competitors to each other in television, and indeed there are a good number of private radio operations and websites that also represent competition. I worked for one of the very first legal commercial radio stations in Britain, LBC. We never had the resources the BBC had, but at least we existed. You wouldn't find LBC-type content in any part of the BBC's portfolio, just as Capital Radio and Radio 1 are very different to each other. That's very healthy – it's the competition Tory politicians think of as essential. It already exists. If you're going to have a market, the whole sector is richer for having both private and public actors in it.

It may be anathema to some, but I am of the unwavering opinion that it is essential to have the BBC, so important to the culture of the land, firmly in the hands of the people. I do not think, therefore, that this is truly a philosophical argument about competition and free enterprise. What, then, is the real reason why some Tory MPs, and indeed some Labour MPs, have a problem with the BBC?

This should be obvious.

The BBC has comprehensive political coverage on a very significant scale. That's healthy for democracy. But it is uncomfortable for politicians, because the media remains the chief mechanism by which they are held to account. Denuding the BBC is, fundamentally, about denuding its capacity to speak truth to power. The BBC is a beacon of hope for millions around the world and one of our greatest cultural exports. To dismantle it for capitalist ideology, or, as I more suspect, so that the British government is held to less rigorous account, would be an act of self-harm. Politicians veer from being more to less likely to give interviews – in the recent period I would regard it as less likely. Former Prime Minister Boris Johnson, for example, who prior to holding the premiership you could hardly restrain from giving an interview, as PM proved harder to obtain. When you can't interview people, it's more difficult to scrutinize them.

Politicians dislike the extent to which the BBC has the capacity to explore and, when necessary, expose. My argument is that if you're not satisfied with the way it's governed, you'll need to make a very good case and have a very open debate about the way in which you would tinker with it to make it acceptable. Otherwise what you have is, ultimately, an attack on an institution upholding a free press. The truly sad thing is that in recent years, politicians on both sides of the aisle have attacked the BBC. I have reserved much of my ire here for Tories because they happen to be in power quite a lot. But when Jeremy Corbyn was the leader of the opposition, BBC journalists came in for a lot of flak. Corbyn was open in his dislike of the media in general, and the BBC in particular. He and his followers expressed a deep suspicion of the media; perhaps unwittingly, they had some interest in a similar sort of control of the media that the Tory

Party had. It's a merciful relief that, despite there being hardliners on both sides of Parliament, they did not get their way on this issue.

Such a situation can often happen when the opposition is out of power for a long time. The Corbynites saw the media as a hindrance to their ambitions. Jeremy Corbyn was ploughing a lonely furrow, and I suspect it was therefore harder to resist paranoid views of media bias. Truthfully, I've never found that British media, as a bloc, has any stance of any sort. Certainly, it would not have been difficult to find journalists who worked at the BBC, and elsewhere, who were personally sympathetic to his brand of socialism – as of course there were Tory sympathisers – even if their reporting was to be governed by the rules of the regulator. As I have written previously, every journalist has a view. I really don't think, therefore, that there existed what Jeremy Corbyn most feared – a closed door, a solid bloc who did not want him to become prime minister.

My guess is that he thought 'we' journalists were against him. But there is no 'we'. The media is a diverse and shifting group of people and interests. As for me personally, I have never been on any side; I only ever want to find out what the truth of the matter is. When I interviewed Jeremy Corbyn, I was trying to find out what he wanted to do. It was hard, as it often is with politicians, to get a clear answer. Nevertheless, it is my duty, as a member of a free press, to ask. And asking was often made extremely difficult, because Corbyn's team made very little effort to contact us, to talk with us, to tell us what they were doing and why. Their lack of willingness to talk with many in the media probably only served to fuel their paranoia. We ended up in a vicious cycle.

The Corbyn leadership of the Labour Party illustrates how things can go wrong if politicians don't want to engage with the media that's paid to report on them. This became destructive because it often looked as if we didn't give them even a fair bite of the cake. But they didn't want to talk to us. I think, just as conceivably, that there are elements of the Conservative Party today who believe in some way that the BBC is ideologically opposed to them; Corbyn felt the same but on the other side of the equation. Of course, if both sides of the aisle think an institution is biased against them, it's probably doing its job. In both instances, Tory and Labour, I cannot help but see the parallel with Iran that began this chapter. Being open with the media allows you to crow about your achievements, to explain your policies, as well as be exposed to criticism. A free press is a tool to be used, not a force to be fought.

I am utterly convinced of the BBC's important place in our news ecosystem, and how it contributes to the existence of a free press. As I argued in the last chapter, needing to turn a profit can skew the way a story is portrayed. Having a news source that is owned by the people, that operates for the people and that is regulated independently to ensure it stays that way is a great boon to our society. It sets us apart from many other countries. We would dearly miss the BBC if we were to lose it.

Attacks on the free press

On Saturday, 20 July 2013, in the basement of the *Guardian*'s London office, under the watchful eye of two GCHQ technicians, three editors destroyed hard drives and memory cards on which encrypted files leaked by Edward Snowden were stored. To quote directly from the newspaper:

> In two tense meetings last June and July the cabinet secretary, Jeremy Heywood, explicitly warned the *Guardian*'s editor, Alan Rusbridger, to return the Snowden documents.
>
> Heywood, sent personally by David Cameron, told the editor to stop publishing articles based on leaked material from America's National Security Agency and GCHQ. At one point Heywood said: 'We can do this nicely or we can go to law.' He added: 'A lot of people in government think you should be closed down.'[1]

The Snowden leaks were about the United States' NSA and GCHQ gathering data from citizens' private digital communications. There had been no consent sought from the public for the appropriation of this data, and to many it felt as though the government had overstepped the mark – it was rather like them opening your mail. Undoubtedly, the case was in the public interest.

And yet the state – the British state – tried to put a stop to a discussion about this once it came to light following Snowden's leaks. When the government starts threatening or mauling a news organization it is treading on very, *very* dangerous ground. We can certainly understand why a communist regime, one which commits to no debate, no passing on of unapproved information, would want to have a newspaper destroy information that it holds. But the idea that a Western democracy found the capacity to do such a thing is amazing. I'm sure a lot of people were very shocked. They should be. It is shocking.

This behaviour is not unique to the Conservatives. Similar abuses have happened under Labour, too, in the dim distance of time. When you get a very long run of one party in power, there is a greater danger that this sort of thing occurs, and it's only after the event that they realize it probably wasn't a very good idea. For one thing, it seems to me the structures are all in place for politicians to challenge journalists and what they do. To move beyond that, to call in the forces of law and order, I think violates the constitutional settlement we have between the media and the government. Our regulatory systems have enshrined the principle that the media should be free to report on matters of public interest – you can't move the goalposts after the fact just because journalists start in on a story that you don't like. At its most basic you are beginning the slow creep towards totalitarianism.

A free press is the driver of freedom at large; the health of our democracy is predicated on the extent to which we can divine the truth, and make our voices heard if we want something changed. Governments, particularly those that are long in the tooth, have a habit of seeking to diminish people's ability to criticize. A perfect contemporary example of this is the new police powers bill, which was brought forward, ultimately, to stop people from protesting. During the Covid-19 pandemic, a wave of protests hit. Some were related to Black Lives Matter, others to violence against women, others still for the perceived attack on civil liberties implied by the lockdowns. The state wished to restrict the public's ability to protest at this time and limit the effective tactics that had been developed, such as the climate activist group Extinction Rebellion's occupation of bridges and roads. Whilst not explicitly a free press issue, it is an example of an assault on freedom of expression. Just like attacks on the free press, it strikes me as a rather cack-handed way of going about things. The mechanics already exist for the police or others to take action during protests to prevent violence and to protect safety. I think the very fact that they didn't want to use the existing powers indicates they were on dodgy ground. It implies that the protesters weren't doing anything wrong, and so creative laws had to be invented to criminalize reasonable behaviour. As citizens we all have a role to play here. These moves are counter-democratic, when we know that there are a lot of very good reasons to live in a democracy. Chief amongst them is the ability to learn from past mistakes. If we shut down the right to make a noise when a mistake has been made, by extension we shut down the ability to improve our society.

All of this weakens and diminishes us. A good government has a mind to improve the way it governs and is not so thin-skinned as to avoid any kind of criticism. Bringing in the military, the intelligence services or the police to 'deal with' protesters and journalists weakens the reputation of and regard for the state – it shows up politicians to be more concerned with saving face than with doing the job they are appointed to. It suggests they have something to hide. Given the level of scrutiny that the Snowden leaks implied the intelligence services put us under, is it not fair that we scrutinize the state just as well?

Integrity

The ability to report the facts without fear or favour is inextricably entwined with the rule of law, which is the very foundation of democracy. Without it, you are rowing into very dark waters. Still, whilst I see a lot of commentary flying about that suggests we are under imminent threat from becoming a dictatorship, or that we have taken a dictatorial turn, I'm not sure that is the case. It's always the prerogative of governments to try to claw back ever more power, and it's a natural instinct for people to try to avoid taking responsibility for their mistakes. I want to conclude this chapter by saying that, despite the attacks I've detailed, we haven't, and we will not, lose our free press as long as the citizenry remains engaged with efforts to discover the truth, and the press continues to deliver the truth to the public.

If you've done nearly half a century of journalism and you come out of it feeling optimistic, you are either a lunatic or, just possibly, you may be right. I think I'm right. Things are getting better, and I reckon they will continue to get better. The information climate that we have today is not, in my view, noticeably more unstable than it was in the past. There's a lot of talk about post-truth politics, and there is plenty of evidence of politicians who lie in public. But a history of the political lie would be a very long book indeed, having to start, I suspect, with ancient Greece and the birth of democracy. In all my time working with politicians, I don't think I have detected any fundamental shift concerning their behaviour and their beliefs. Rather, I think we are now more aware than at any other time of bad behaviour, and politicians are, more often than not, being held to account. Whilst we may feel depressed by the state of our leaders, whilst we may feel that there is not enough consequence, we are on the right trajectory. Previous eras had fewer scandals *because they got away with them*. They get away with it far more seldom today. There's progress and, despite the many challenges and drawbacks it has brought, social media has been one of the forces that has brought pressure to bear on Parliament, and helped move it into the twenty-first century.

Far older than social media, though, is our regulatory system. The regulator helps our free press flourish; it doesn't strangle it as some claim. I have never found myself going to bed at night after a hard day saying, 'Bugger the regulations.' No, I think the equilibrium we have struck, which has emerged over decades, is good. I also can't say that I've struggled to respect the regulatory framework or to make use of it. Relatively recently, I was investigated by Ofcom for a broadcast I did covering a Brexit protest. I said, 'It has been the most extraordinary day . . . A day which has seen – I've never seen so many white people in one place. It's an extraordinary story. There are people everywhere, there are crowds everywhere.' Some people complained that this showed a bias and the regulator looked into it. In the end, Ofcom found that I had not been in breach of the broadcasting code, and we all moved on. I'm glad people were able to air their concerns, I'm glad that they were taken seriously, and I'm glad that my conduct was held to the high standard that people expect. In this instance, it was no harm, no foul – I knew it would be because I have worked alongside this regulatory system for my entire broadcasting life. Regulators seem to me to be relatively uncontroversial. If governments or citizens have criticisms about reporting, there is a channel that already exists through which those criticisms can go. Regulation means that we don't broadcast hate speech, but that, at the same time, we strike a balance with what we put on air. This is a responsible way to govern a free press. What we don't need is new rules that go above and beyond the regulatory system that currently exists.

Nevertheless, these things – maintaining independent regulation and social media – do present a challenge. We must be alert to threats and push back against any erosion of our right to report the news.

When I saw the tragedy of Iran – a wonderful culture hamstrung by its lack of a free press – I saw the limits of journalism. I fear that change in Iran – a rebalancing of the power dynamic between the religious and military elites and the mass of the people being brought about by journalism – is unlikely. Uncensored news creeps in, and perhaps this slow drip will eventually create a dam-breaking force. But, at least for the time being, the unequal, totalitarian society seems likely to remain, which makes it all the more remarkable that there are those brave individuals who talk to the foreign press.

What we can do to honour our brave Iranian counterparts, and people like them in places where the free press is non-existent, is protect and renew our British institutions. We let them perish at our peril. They are – as I hope this chapter has convinced you – critical to the survival of democracy and to the integrity of news reporting. Without a free press, it is impossible for journalists to do their job properly, and when they don't, democracy atrophies. I think our democracy is robust enough to assist in this: that all parties and actors do actually believe in a free press, even if they disagree about what it might look like. As citizens and as journalists, this act of maintenance is a cardinal responsibility for us.

And I mention citizens as well as journalists because the citizenry – meaning all of us – does have a role to play in the maintenance of our democracy, not in an abstract way, but in a very concrete one. One of the truths of a democracy is that what you do in life, right down to keeping yourself informed, actually matters. You have the power, by being informed, by pursuing the truth, to make yourself heard – on the streets, in the ballot box, or even just amongst your friends and family and community. What people say, what they think and what they do, makes a difference to collective life.

And it is the same sense of making a difference, that mission-based purpose, that should be at the heart of journalistic life. The most important word in the whole equation is this: integrity. Nobody can brag that every journalist tells the truth all the time – just look at Boris Johnson – but collectively we can endeavour to stick to the truth and defend the truth whenever it's under siege.

Integrity to me means honesty. It must therefore, to some extent, also mean objectivity. It means trust. And, above all, it means hope. Hope that we have the integrity to see off our demons. As I come towards the end of my career, I hope that I have been as truthful and as honest as a journalist can be. But the beauty of the model we have is that it is for others to judge. Integrity is not a quality I can profess to having: integrity is a quality that others can see, not one that you inculcate in a vacuum. That means that, just as I turn the spotlight on politicians, the citizenry can turn the spotlight me as a journalist. Integrity means remaining open to the processes that we bring to bear on others.

After all, how are we going to get better if we do not know what it is that we're doing wrong?

CHAPTER 8

THE NEXT GENERATION

I GOT TO THE ISSUE terribly late in my career; I should
have thought of it a lot earlier. By 2018, though, it was
impossible not to be aware of the gender pay gap issues
across our industry. Even those who partnered with me
to anchor Channel 4 News were victims of discrimination. Despite having similar tasks, despite often being
better qualified – with better exam results and better
degrees – women were paid less than me.

Truthfully, I was concerned when I started to consider
what to do about it. I thought that reducing my income
was the right thing to do, but on the other hand I had
developed a lifestyle that required the pay I was getting –
chief amongst my worries was my rather costly mortgage.
I wanted to do something, but I knew, too, that it was
going to entail some sort of personal sacrifice. Clearly, I
was not about to become destitute, but the move required
consideration on my part. In the end, I recognized that
there was a campaign on gender pay and, whilst I
wouldn't say I was a force within it, I wanted to voice my
opinions on it.

I believe that what we do matters. That's particularly true if you manage to get yourself into a position of influence. In such a case, you have an obligation to others. You must, at the very least, set an example by advocating for better conditions for the people you work with. That is what I believe, what I have always believed, and that meant that I could not stand by and be the beneficiary of so blatant an injustice. So I took a significant pay cut.

I'm not trying to come over as grand or saintly; I don't want a pat on the back for this. Whilst it came at a financial cost, there was no suggestion that I was going to be sacked or anything like that. I was at no real personal risk. Besides which, I felt as though I was just heading off a problem that was bound to come around eventually. Equalizing pay is inevitable, logical and reasonable. You can't go on educating women to the same level as men and then say, 'The equality ends when you leave university. You don't need to be treated the same when you enter the workplace.' Clearly, that's not going to work. The media is probably, in terms of gender, one of the most integrated industries, but it remains unintegrated when it comes to being paid fairly for the work you do. And, in many respects, pay disparity is just the tip of the iceberg.

I have never thought that every worker in an organization should be paid exactly the same. As an anchor, there is a voice in your ear coming from the director and the timekeeper. They give instructions as to what you are supposed to be doing. These are directives that you trust implicitly, and the people offering them are essential to the broadcasting of the news every night. I don't think I am prepared to see the timekeeper paid as much as the presenter, yet no timekeeper should be paid more than another because of their gender. Likewise, it seemed to me that some roles have, certainly historically, been taken predominantly by men. When I travelled with a crew, women were under-represented in some jobs – camera operators, sound people. Why? A woman could operate a camera as well as a man. What was going on? As with all inequality, once you start seeing it, it becomes increasingly hard to unsee it.

Great changes have taken place over the course of my lifetime. It was not that long ago when there were extraordinarily few women in journalism. In the early part of my career, I never worked alongside women. I had also not been to school with women, or grown up amongst them. Women were significantly less a part of public life at the time. As times changed, women have taken up ever greater positions of authority. One of the most remarkable women that I ever worked with, indeed one of the most remarkable people, was Diana Edwards-Jones. She was an absolutely class director. The whole look of News at Ten, when I worked there as a reporter, was created by her, not by a man. Today, thankfully, there is an even greater shift towards balance. So much of what you see on television is shaped by women, both behind and in front of the camera – female producers, designers, directors, all of them with huge ability. Yet still many are not paid the same rate as men. Things are changing, but this is a problem across our society. I don't think for one minute that individual men collude so that they get paid more than women. Like the other equality problems in this book, it is a structural one and it will need a structural solution.

I was prominent in my support of equalizing pay but, as I said, I was rather late to the party. I hope it helped to have me putting a shoulder to the wheel. But, equally, I didn't go out campaigning on the street. I didn't write articles for newspapers; I wasn't spending my days banging this drum. The campaign had been started by women many decades prior, and it wasn't until 2018 that the government, under pressure from campaign groups, themselves amplified by the news media, forced companies to publish their pay gaps. I never would have taken a pay cut were it not for the increasingly active campaigning of others. Back in the 1970s, when I was working in that hugely male-dominated era of journalism, we were not regularly running stories about the gender pay gap. It wasn't on the radar of most of the men I worked with. It certainly wasn't on my radar. But it was still a problem. Women were not being paid the same as men back then and, indeed, the workplace was significantly more hostile towards them in general.

Journalism, the free flow of information, led to the issue becoming salient. If more women hadn't entered the news workforce, would the issue have risen up the reporting agenda? Would it have made its way into the legislative agenda? Would it have entered the water-cooler conversations of ordinary people in their workplaces up and down the country? I doubt it.

This is a perfect example of why equality, in the broadest possible sense, is crucial when establishing the journalistic workforce. And it's also why journalism, unwittingly, has at times helped entrench or reflect the inequality it should have exposed.

Journalism and diversity

Representation matters. That's true in every field. However, the people who make the news also make choices about what constitutes news. Reporting on wider society, we should reflect it too. When we don't understand equality, when we aren't mindful of the issues that affect our status in society – men and women, Black and white, rich and poor – we are less able to do that. This chapter is about diversity, and my hopes for ever-increasing amounts of it. It is about the new generation of journalists entering the workforce. It is, ultimately, about equality of opportunity in the newsroom, where it exists, where it doesn't, and why it's important.

When we think about diversity, we very often leap straight into classifying people. We talk about diversity of races, genders and classes. This is all well and good, but it misses the most crucial element of diversity, the fruit, if you will. Having diversity in a workplace is about a group of different personalities, experiences and outlooks, all rowing together to make something brilliant. The reason to do so in journalism is exemplified by the change I detailed above.

If you have a news corps that reflects the society they're reporting on, they're more likely to find stories from across that society. That was true of women from the early 1970s: those female journalists were spotting things that men hadn't yet woken up to – men were not seeing and experiencing what they were seeing and experiencing. Once women started bringing in new types of stories, it took commitment from the whole team to create space for them within the broadcast, for all of us to broaden our outlook, and for all of us to fight to have unheard voices aired.

Often this comes about through simple conversation with others. My thinking around equality, and my approach to journalism, is shaped less by reading big, thick academic tomes and much more by people coming up to me and talking about their experiences. There are many intimate moments in television production. One is editing at a video console. It's just you, the producer and the editor. It could be the case that, out of the three, I am the only male. Depending on the issue we are working on, very fertile conversations are possible.

For instance, when we were attempting to cover Mrs Thatcher, I can remember us often getting into rich conversation about whether she was, or was not, a feminist. The question might have been raised between colleagues – male and female – over whether Thatcher understood women's rights. At the time I contended that, to some extent, she did, but at the same time she had other priorities which played more strongly in her heart. I think most of the men I worked with may well have thought the same thing, and, perhaps like me, they may not have spent a huge amount of time thinking about it beyond that. But it could be in one of those moments at the video console that the film editor would perhaps pipe up and say, 'Thatcher, I don't think she cares a damn about women.' It was impossible to shut that out.

It sounds so straightforward as to be almost bathetic, but having women around changed the way we covered the first female prime minister. If it had been ten, twenty years prior, I am not sure I can, hand on heart, say that when I interviewed her I would have asked her about women's opportunities. The fact of her presence in the highest office of the land seemed to suggest that women had all the rights that men did. But the conversations that we were having back at the studio forced me to interrogate the situation much more deeply than I otherwise would have done.

Of course, Thatcher always gave a very fluid but bland answer to such a question. As it turns out, I don't think we can say that she was a raging feminist. When I asked her if she defined herself as such, she sort of turned up her nose. She was very much of the 'If I can get here, anyone can' school of thought. But this was, in itself, fascinating. The fact that this was how she viewed *this* particular issue gave us a rare insight into how she viewed many others. Whilst it's hard to know how deeply she analysed her own attitudes to a whole range of things, I'm sure the 'If I can get here, anyone can' mentality was of a piece with her philosophy as a whole – she never really looked at systemic issues. She always believed primarily in the ability and power of the individual. Questioning her on the issue of women's rights and feminism proved far more fertile than I could have imagined.

Thatcher is a single instance, though. I don't think any outsider coming in over the years would have said, 'Gosh, there's a great debate about feminism over at ITN.' If anything, I now look back with a certain amount of guilt. I could have worked harder at highlighting these kinds of issues at the time. But then I wanted to get to the top. I wanted to become an anchor. These things were in competition with each other. You didn't want to become known as a troublemaker. I had a reputation for a very minor amount of troublemaking, only ever a bit. This was considered healthy. To be very much a troublemaker, that would be a nuisance. This story tells a much wider truth – for change to happen, you need people to actually *do* something. We may all agree that there really ought to be equal pay, but it's very easy for us to say that and then twiddle our thumbs. If we're going to foster diversity, we can't all stand on the sidelines. I'm glad, therefore, that I took the pay cut – I just wish I had done more sooner. Not least because, in a very minor sense, I am a beneficiary of people not standing on the sidelines. Lots of people took chances with me as a young journalist. And

I was not, in every way, exactly what you might expect them to be looking for.

I knew I had a capacity for hard work, it's just that hard work in the academic setting produced for me rather measly O-Level and A-Level results. Nevertheless, I was happy to embrace the twelve- and fourteen-hour days that were the norm at ITN when I started out. Sometimes we would go for forty-eight hours without sleep. I would drive or fly huge distances, live away from friends and family for months at a time. It was full on. I was willing to sacrifice my personal life for my career – people suffered at my hand, relationships fell apart because I was never there. That was tough. At the same time, I have to admit that I found the lifestyle hugely enjoyable and rewarding. It was exhausting, but I loved every minute of it.

I don't think I am unintelligent. But I'd be wrong not to reflect that, as a child, and as I advanced through my career, I did feel a sense of inadequacy because many of my peers were scholars. They were high-grade. The media had the pick; they had whoever they wanted. To survive in journalism, I knew I had to be very good at the job because I lacked some of my rivals' natural intellect. The era of media in which I began my career, though, was what people used to call a 'kick bollock and scramble' situation. You would hear a piece of information. You'd ring somebody up, you'd drive over to them, you'd book a plane, you'd grab your crew, you'd wine and dine and cajole, reprimand or charm. You'd do, in short, anything and everything to get that story and deliver it back to the team at the office with time to spare. You can't teach that. Not entirely. Being an enormous intellect doesn't necessarily help you with it. Mine is a more animal intelligence rather than the bookish sort of some of my peers. But it was an intelligence that, I believe, enriched our newsroom. In the round, it wasn't to my detriment that I am not one of life's natural scholars – it was to my advantage, and to the advantage of my colleagues who were different from me. Equally, it was essential that our newsroom also had people with fantastic minds, whose knowledge of a very specific subject enhanced our reporting.

Bringing different types of intelligence together is challenging, exciting and, in the end, hugely positive. It meant that, whilst I may not have known about the political economy of tractor manufacturing in Slovakia between the end of the Soviet Union and that nation's integration into the EU, I had a colleague who did. On the other hand, this learned colleague may not have been fully comfortable walking into a factory outside of Prešov and striking up a conversation with a mechanic of fifty years' experience, whereas I am at ease in such a situation. Our different experiences and personalities allow us to pull a much richer story together than if we were working individually. This is the point of diversity. It's not simply a nice thing to have. It's not an exercise in political correctness. It's a logical, time-honoured way to improve what you're doing. And that's true in every field from journalism to . . . tractor manufacturing.

That means we have a challenge on our hands. We are reaching the culmination of the argument that this book has been making. Combatting inequality of opportunity and economic inequality and combatting inequality in the newsroom go hand in hand. A diverse staff will be alive to an abundance of stories that a narrow band of people simply will not. This creates a virtuous circle. The public then become more informed about those stories, and in my view, when armed with the truth, the public tend to make pretty rational choices about how they want to live. If ignorance is the driver of inequality, journalism is the best device we have to inform and educate. Education begets change, and the key measure of this change is economic.

It's difficult to have an objective perspective on the present, but there are signs that, as it stands, the media is not diverse enough by half. My fear is that the public may have been somewhat misinformed as a result.

If you had said in 2015 that, in fewer than five years, Boris Johnson would be the prime minister, and that he would have prorogued Parliament to take Britain out of the EU, no journalist would have taken you seriously. Journalists were, in the main, too busy frothily reporting the Chinese economic miracle to see the potential for a pandemic like Covid-19 to spread rapidly around our globalized world. Vladimir Putin was merely 'sabre-rattling' when he massed tanks on the border of Ukraine in January 2022.

And then there was Grenfell.

It is at least worth considering whether huge stories such as Grenfell or Brexit would have been reported on differently if the workforce was more engaged and representative of the people who were involved. Eventually, we ended up with very good reporting and a much closer view of the facts in both instances. But it took us a long time. After all, the Grenfell fire was in 2017. It's an unbelievable thought that the truth is still being unravelled to this very day – five full years as I write. We began work on it the very night it happened, and I had the sense when I was there that we were dealing with an epoch-defining moment. Grenfell was a truly British catastrophe, an event in which immigrants and the working classes were the victims of the negligence of the rich and powerful. It is perhaps not a surprising conclusion. What is surprising is that it's taken us half a decade to clarify quite how much went wrong, and how.

At the time of the fire, there were flashing warning signs that something was amiss. But the media overlooked them. I could feel, in those initial hours, that there was a scandal. What should be shocking is not that it had been covered up – largely, it hadn't been. It is much worse than that. It had gone unnoticed. It had gone unnoticed by us in the media. It is a journalist's job, by definition, to know what is going on. We didn't know. We didn't have the connections with the kinds of people who were the victims of the tragedy. They couldn't get in touch with us. They didn't send snippets on Twitter; they weren't directing the online conversation.

The people living in the tower, some without access to computers or smartphones, were too busy struggling with the matters of everyday life for the problems they faced to be picked up in the news. We journalists had become disconnected from a section of society, and this odious breakdown meant that the lever we can pull to prevent such a tragedy was left untouched. It was only after the fire that journalists learnt of Edward Daffarn, a fifty-five-year-old social worker who had lived on the estate for sixteen years. He had written a blog which showed with prophetic clarity the many failings of the council in providing adequate fire precautions. It is all very well saying that the structures were in place – that the journalist's door is open, as is the local MP's at surgery hour, or indeed that people can organize their own protest and march through the streets – but, I'm sorry, the average citizen living in Grenfell Tower, raising a family, working an exhausting job, was not free to use them. And when they did, as in Daffarn's case, nobody paid enough attention.

Grenfell happened just after the media had received its shock on Brexit. All the predictions at the time had put Remain on course for a slim but comfortable (and comforting) win. It was profusely clear in the months afterwards that the media were simply not listening to constituent parts of the country. Clear divides, ancient fronts ever present in British politics – between country and city, north and south, working-class and professional – were unearthed during the campaign. But they had little to do with the matter at hand. From beginning to end, from top to bottom (and particularly to the bottom, because it is the poorest in our society who will suffer most as a result), Brexit has been a complete scandal. A tiny minority of people used their political position and their clout to bring about something that, in all conscience, I don't think the electorate was equipped to make a judgement on.

The class system in Britain is very much intact. It has changed, but it shows no sign of withering. Inequality is still the key issue of the day. You cannot ask an unequal society to make so big a judgement on such a complicated issue. That's what you elect governments to do. Referenda, generally speaking – and history is largely on my side – are dangerous weapons, especially in the wrong hands. Simply put, a referendum in an unequal society will merely reflect the unfairness of that society, and not some amorphous 'will of the people'.

But the media itself is part of this class problem. I think we must give the media its due, somewhat. I have already mentioned that it was a very, very difficult issue to report on. There was a populist movement to take us out of Europe, one that weaponized people's economic precarity to achieve the unrelated end of Brexit. None of us in the highly regulated world of broadcast media wanted to be accused of playing a role in influencing the referendum one way or the other: our job is to be as impartial as possible. Therefore journalists were, I believe, shy of interrogating both sides of the referendum question as vigorously as they might have done. It was a very delicate time; none of us wanted to be caught with our pants down. On the other hand, I think large sectors of the print media did play a significant role in swinging the referendum.

Still, I do not believe any part of the media appreciated the scale of the citizenry's economic woes, or how the years of reducing the welfare state had led to a more fractured society. This inability to see was, in part, down to a failure to diversify the newsroom. There are far fewer people in journalism drawn from parts of the country that voted to leave the EU – places like Middlesbrough or Cornwall – and those that are, very often, did not attend a state school.

In both cases, Grenfell and Brexit, having a greater plurality of people working in journalism would have improved our access to the real story – to the stark economic inequality, to the chronic inequality of opportunity. There is a vicious cycle at play. Economic inequality leads to inequality of opportunity, and, with time, that drives ever fewer of the people the newsroom desperately needs to a job in journalism. I know there must be many talented young people who are put off because they don't think that they have the necessary experience or education or are simply not the right 'sort' for the job. If you don't see people who look or sound like you doing the job of a journalist, you may conclude that people who look or sound like you don't become journalists. This means that we lose people before they even start – they never apply.

The prize is a world in which the people making the broadcast are similar to the people consuming it. We are far from this. Simply by looking at education, we can see that the proportion of people who went to public school or Oxbridge and work in the media, particularly in senior positions, is eye-watering. Of the people who made up the News Media 100 in 2019, the most influential people in news, 43 per cent went to a private school;[1] 44 per cent of newspaper columnists went to a private school. A further 36 per cent of people in the News Media 100 went to Oxbridge, as did 44 per cent of columnists. The percentage of people in the country as a whole who attended a private school is 7 per cent; the percentage of people who went to Oxbridge is less than 1 per cent.[2] This should outrage us. Furthermore, the media is significantly behind the other institutions of the elite, too: 27 per cent of FTSE 350 company CEOs attended a private school, and 28 per cent of the *Sunday Times* Rich List did. Twenty per cent of our pop stars went to a private school, and 31 per cent of our Olympic medallists.[3] None of these figures should make us feel proud, but they represent a better social mix than in my own industry. Class determines so much in our society, and change is not going to happen overnight. It's very difficult to achieve, but – to improve the quality of our broadcasting, to get a better handle on the issues of the day and to leave our viewers and readers informed – I believe our media must reflect the society we actually live in.

It's all well and good us thinking about this from a purely businesslike perspective. I think there is a strong case that diversity in the newsroom will make for a better media, one more adept in its pursuit of truth. But it's not simply about that for me. There is an emotional component to this, too. It ties in with what I wrote at the beginning of this book, something I fervently believe: the key to living a good life is the ability to live harmoniously with other people. That harmony can be more difficult to achieve when you live amongst people who are ostensibly very different to you; perhaps you want different things. But it also has the potential to be more rewarding. I so fervently believe this because it was a lesson I learnt at such a formative age in Uganda – whilst it was imperfect, our little community, made up of very different people, really worked, and really enriched my life.

When we think of workplaces, they can sometimes seem separate from society at large and from our communities. But I think community is at the heart of all life, including our working life. It's my wish not simply that the media has X per cent of people represented in Y roles. Our media landscape must have a common understanding that allows everybody, from varied backgrounds, to work together. There have been moments in my career when that has happened. My time at Channel 4 was a happy one, particularly the last few years. A community environment existed there. It wasn't down to me: a lot of different people were involved in creating that kind of atmosphere. But I basked in it. I really enjoyed it.

It's this community spirit that is essential for developing the career of a young journalist. I didn't rely on it so much when I started out, though it is worth reflecting on what my public-school education really gave me in my career. Arrogance. My class gave me an utterly undeserved arrogance. We were treated differently from the average person. There was a certain sense of superiority instilled in us. It left me able to ignore my serious shortcomings and free to blunder about making my way. I was able to learn gradually on the job without losing the job in the process. The latitude I was given, whilst won without merit, was immensely useful to me. Not every young person entering the media has the good fortune to feel so sure of themselves, and that makes them less able to make mistakes. But mistakes are essential. They are how we learn. The upshot of being so self-assured was a certain degree of imperviousness. Such imperviousness should be extended to all those entering the media landscape, even if their ego and confidence are not so vast as mine. The mistakes we make early on in our careers are our greatest educators. Yet if you feel so grateful to have managed to get your foot in the door, you may feel too nervous ever to make such a mistake. Where people don't have the arrogance gifted by a public school, they must be nurtured.

It's clear, then, that if we are to diversify the new talent coming into journalism, certain people are going to need more support: for some, it will be a more foreign experience than for others. Everybody has a role to play in creating this kind of community environment in their workplace. As for me, I felt the least I could do was to try to make myself available. I never lingered long on the pedestal you inevitably occupy in the newsroom when you're the presenter. The benefits of doing this, for me, cut both ways. I enjoyed talking to people from different backgrounds. Seeing new journalists grow was one of the most rewarding elements of my working life, and is one of the reasons I was drawn to journalism in the first place. I enjoy talking to people who have a different view, who have lived a different life experience to my own. In other words, I enjoy diversity.

Whether we are talking about class, ethnicity, religion, gender, nationality or something else, all these aspects play a part in the life of an individual, and they should be seen as strengths that can be brought to bear on the wider news ecosystem. Sometimes I get the sense that people feel disheartened, or that there has been no progress on these issues. I can understand why – the figures I quoted above are, as I said, eye-watering. And yet, given the changes I have witnessed across my working life, I feel a great sense of optimism. I have a strong belief that we are moving in the right direction. In the 1980s, for instance, the newsroom was significantly whiter, more male and more middle-class. I think Britain, per se, was far less aware of issues of gender and ethnicity in those times. At the time, were a Black woman to be overlooked for a position because of the colour of her skin, I suspect there would have been very little outrage. Today, that kind of overt discrimination is anathema to us. We are not perfect, but I'm glad that we are at least aboard the train, and I'm excited to see where it will take us.

Celebrating multiculturalism

There has been a huge change in the demographic make-up of Britain over the course of my life. I fear that, too often, we talk negatively about our multicultural society, yet it is one of our greatest assets as a country. I want to conclude this chapter by saying that what is true of the newsroom is true of society at large. Diversity is a fantastic driver of innovation and growth – it makes the place we live in, the community we foster, better. Our diverse and multicultural society is a clear and untrammelled good. It isn't perfect by any means, but it feels like we rarely celebrate what has been a massive transformation over the past half-century.

On just one front of diversity, there is immigration, and immigrants have tremendously enhanced our society. Migrants have renovated and empowered this nation in ways that few of us could have predicted. They have become a part of the fabric of our society, and we are a richer, more luxuriant tapestry as a result. In my youth, even though there were significant numbers of migrants here, I didn't come across them. They didn't teach me at school; I didn't see them on television. Growing up, we had only the very vaguest sense that people were coming from the Caribbean. Certainly, there were not vast numbers of the recently arrived in mid-Sussex. I remember the first Black person I met was at a printing shop near my home – he worked there. The idea that, within my lifetime, Caribbean immigrants or their children would enter the House of Lords, would be running major businesses, or, indeed, would anchor the evening news was unthinkable. Yet it has come to pass. I don't think any of us are under the illusion that Britain is some kind of racial utopia – but, by the same token, these changes take place by accretion, and that takes time.

I'm hugely in favour of immigration and the changes it has brought to Britain. Truthfully, I think that white Britain needed diversifying – cultures and nations thrive on change and evolution. The society I grew up in was tired and stale. The one I live in now has, despite its many problems, an energy and liveliness to it. I can only conclude that immigration has immensely enriched us. Most obviously, there are the economic terms in which this is provably and demonstrably the case. It is extremely well documented that there is an entrepreneurial spirit amongst many immigrant businesspeople: immigrants massively outperform native-born Britons as entrepreneurs. According to research by the think tank The Entrepreneurs Network, whilst just 14 per cent of UK residents are foreign-born, 49 per cent of the UK's fastest-growing businesses have at least one foreign-born founder.

In fact, nine out of the UK's fourteen start-up 'unicorns' (a privately held entity valued at over \$1 billion) have at least one immigrant co-founder, including big hitters like Wise and OakNorth; they hail from twenty-nine different countries all over the world, from the USA and France to Lebanon and Kyrgyzstan.[4] Just as diversity is the key to a good news report, so too is it the key to our continued prosperity and global competitiveness.

Despite such obvious success stories, I fear that the conversation we have around immigration is very often not positive or supportive. In fact, it is at times offensive, sometimes even frightening. There are an awful lot of white working-class people who feel insecure about immigration for a variety of reasons. Chief amongst them is the fear that people have joined the British job market who might be willing to work for less. There is also the concern that, as public resources – the NHS, the welfare state, council houses – become increasingly scarce, immigrants may be given special treatment, or take up a valued slot in a zero-sum game. These fears may be ill-founded, but they are fears nevertheless. An obvious way in which to alleviate them would be to make public services more accessible, and bolster protections in the labour market – for both immigrants and British-born workers. Still, there are tensions. When you add to this mix very unpleasant rhetoric from certain quarters, it is highly destructive and wholly uncalled for.

Still, in the city that I live in, London, it is impossible to ignore the very many beautiful examples of successful migrants and successful integration. I found it cheering to see our Muslim mayor attending a Jewish Seder, reaching across cultures with sympathy and understanding – simple British values like decency and respect go a long way. I feel patriotic when my compatriots demonstrate them. The way in which barriers have been broken down over the course of my lifetime is truly remarkable. As immigrants settle in Britain, as they make lives and start families, they become British themselves. The British identity is strong in part because it is fluid. Despite right-wing protestations to the contrary, there is no subject in Britain today that is a 'no-go' area. Yes, we have problems – the London riots, sparked by the shooting of Mark Duggan by the police, were not all that long ago. But I've lived through much bumpier times than we are in now, and in much bumpier places around the world, too.

I remember Enoch Powell and his 1968 'Rivers of Blood' speech. In it, Powell claimed that allowing people from the Commonwealth to live here and contribute to our economy was an 'insane' act akin to building a 'funeral pyre' for the nation. That kind of politics was quite mainstream. There were plenty of respectable people who apparently thought it a commendable intervention. There is no real equivalent to it today. It is possible that certain people may wish to give a 'Rivers of Blood'-style speech, but they know that they wouldn't get away with it. They have resorted to the dog whistle; they may be blowing that whistle very hard, but the fact that they must resort to an underhand tactic shows how much times have changed. It is my very sincere hope that the country has moved on from an era in which out-and-out racist thinking will gain any real purchase with the population. I believe it's too late to reawaken the racial tiger in this country. I hope I'm not being naïve about this. It is an issue of personal importance to me. I have a Black wife; I have a mixed-race child. As I write, he is still a baby. But as he grows and develops, I hope that it will be in a Britain where the Enoch Powells of our society have been put very firmly back in their box.

My sense is that in my son's lifetime, there won't be a family, workplace, school or community in this country that won't count amongst it somebody who isn't white, or that won't contain people who have recently arrived to our shores. Even as it stands today, it's unusual to find any significant sector of society with no migrant representation, or no ethnic diversity, within it. That changes the way our conversations run. When I look back, my childhood was dominated by class. By whiteness. The choir that I was in had sixteen boys – the line-up was constantly evolving, some moved on, some moved in, but there were never fewer than sixteen. None of them was ever an immigrant. All of them were white. I can't imagine that would be true today. Even in this most rarefied of environments, things have started to change.

In my own field of journalism, there has been a significant shift. As I write, Clive Myrie of the BBC is reporting the evening news every night from Kyiv in Ukraine. To have an authoritative, respected correspondent who happens to be Black in a major war zone *is* remarkable. Sixty years ago, I doubt people would have thought it possible. That a BBC evening television news show would be regularly presented by a Black person, or a Muslim, or a woman with a regional accent was out of the question. It was all men, all white, all privately educated. Today, the people who populate these roles on television has significantly changed and this has been, most of the time, happily accepted by the British people. I don't feel that people are sitting at home en masse saying, 'Dear oh dear, she's not very good, is she?'

I understand that Clive Myrie receives racist abuse, and that the amount of abuse he receives has been increasing in recent years.[5] I suspect that there are three reasons driving this behaviour. The first is that as racist beliefs become increasingly fringe and impotent, the minority who holds them grows increasingly vocal. The next is that social media has allowed a greater level of access to people in the public eye than ever before, and, by extension, has licensed people to communicate with them. The third is that progress does not occur in a linear way. We have been through a polarized time, there have been attempts to stir up resentments, and it is inevitable that these have partially succeeded. The abuse Myrie receives shocks and saddens me. It must be fought at every stage. Nevertheless, it should not detract from the fact that Myrie, the son of Jamaican immigrants, is on our screens every night. He is offering fantastic reporting from

Ukraine, and is unquestionably a broadcaster of the very highest calibre. He is one of the stars of his generation, a boon to my industry and to the civic health of our nation. His success is no doubt down in large part to his own effort and determination, yet it is a success that all of us should celebrate.

Data supports my intuition. In 1983, more than half of respondents to the British Social Attitudes survey expressed discomfort at the idea of a close relative marrying a Black or Asian person. By 2013, this proportion had sharply dropped, and, amongst people born since 1980, only 14 per cent expressed discomfort.[6] Yes, 14 per cent is 14 per cent too many. But the data shows prejudice going from the default position of the average citizen to a view held by a minority in just twenty years. Imagine where we will be in another twenty years. I think it is inconceivable that children born since 2000 will be more racially prejudiced than people who are currently in middle age. This is not to say that all is well, that we have achieved some sort of racial end point. The purpose of this book is to point out inequalities, and when it comes to race or immigration, there are copious issues to address. There are injustices to root out. I have already mentioned Black Lives Matter; it's a tragedy that people need to be reminded that Black lives do indeed matter in this simplistic sense, but I don't think it's anachronistic to do so. There are huge issues for us to overcome, but the fact that we are, increasingly, an integrated society tells me that they are not insurmountable. The fact that there is evidence of improvement over the course of my lifetime should spur us on.

We are, always, a work in progress, and it's for that reason that the way we represent ourselves matters. How we represent ourselves becomes, ultimately, how we understand ourselves. It is who we are. My support for diversity is not simply the morally right position, though it is; it is also a recognition of the great benefits that diversity has brought to Britain. Immigration has improved our society, and the proof of that is in our multicultural pudding. There is no time I would rather live in than now – I have no wish to retreat into the past. It has been a thrill to see our multicultural society emerge, and it remains a thrill to be a part of it.

CONCLUSION

BEING BRAVE

I HAVE HAD THE GOOD fortune to meet and observe many of Britain's leaders. In doing so, I've had the opportunity to investigate the heart of the British establishment, and the psychology at play in high office. This is a journalist's job, of course, but being so near to power creates certain risks. You must get as close as you can to report the story, whilst maintaining a safe enough distance to do so objectively.

Though I met Harold Macmillan, as I have already observed, I was too young to understand either his position or his capacity as prime minister. Looking back, he seemed to have been elevated to his position by the class system rather than by any outstanding political capacity.

I never met Winston Churchill, nor set eyes upon him in the flesh, but his funeral had a huge impact upon me. I was fifteen and at school in Oxford. The ceremony in St Paul's Cathedral on 30 January 1965 was an immense occasion. When the funeral cortège set off for the burial at Bladon, near Oxford, we lined the railway at Port Meadow on the edge of our school. As the simple wagon bearing his coffin and a small guard of honour passed, I, like many others, burst into tears. We had a sense even then that history and greatness were passing, and we were overwhelmed by the emotion of the moment. I was born after the war, yet I had a partial understanding of his role and his singular moment in history. I felt something similar when seeing the TV report of President Kennedy's assassination in Texas in 1963.

I was lucky enough to interview James Callaghan when he was prime minister. I was a young reporter, chuffed to be inside Number Ten. He played the game; he was avuncular and rarely gave much away.

As mentioned, I interviewed Margaret Thatcher a number of times down the years and enjoyed the process hugely. It was both combative and seductive. She didn't like what she full well suspected were my politics, but she seemed to like me all the same. Whilst she was deeply serious, she wasn't above being flirtatious to get her own way, which tied the interviewer in knots. I was a diplomatic correspondent at the time and too often I was her victim. Few of us who interviewed her got the better of her.

John Major was more relaxed, and again I think we had a good, mutually respectful relationship across the microphone.

Tony Blair had all the kit required to be a good prime minister – looks, speaking skills and more. He was effective to interview and sometimes rewarding, but he evaded questions deftly and, in the end, he also evaded becoming one of the great British prime ministers. He will be remembered for failure in Iraq, and not achievements at home.

Gordon Brown I respected. I admired his intellect and his genuine regard for the neglected, and his concern about the abiding issue of inequality. I regarded him as one of the most decent individuals to reach the premiership; he may have suffered for being so.

David Cameron was both suave and an effective leader and a good interviewee. He dealt with questions head on and didn't appear to mind a tough one. It's remarkable that such a capable man ruined his own political future and legacy by calling the Brexit referendum.

Theresa May, on the other hand, was a trifle brittle to interview and not the easiest person to put at ease. It is hard to credit her with any defining policy beyond her abiding commitment to the Conservative Party and all its works.

Which leaves Boris Johnson and the numerous scandals that swirled around him, not least that of Partygate – partying whilst the country was in lockdown. The miracle about him is less that he ever became prime minister than that he managed to remain in position for so long – three years.

Enter Liz Truss. Her campaign propelled a relatively inexperienced minister for foreign affairs into Number 10. Although she had served as foreign secretary, it was only fairly recently that she was talked up as a possible prime minister. A good number of Conservatives were doubtful that she was the right choice, but a good number of others clearly couldn't contemplate the possibility of Rishi Sunak, who had been chancellor of the exchequer until Johnson's downfall. Optimists hoped that this was not due to a reluctance to see a person of colour becoming the British prime minister. When it came to the vote of the Conservative Party members across the country, Liz Truss prevailed, but only a third of the 365 Tory MPs voted for her – hardly a parliamentary vote of confidence. She had not been foreign secretary for long enough ever to be truly tested. Appointed prime minister in a moment of profound crisis for which she was ill prepared, she quickly became the shortest serving prime minister in our country's history, with the Conservatives appointing Rishi Sunak, who had lost the members' vote, to lead the country after all.

I would love to be able to tell you what happens next, but it is impossible to hit a moving target. We are reaching the conclusion of this book, just as I am coming to the end of my career. I have no plans to hang up my boots yet, but I am aware that there are a greater number of years' reporting behind me than there are ahead of me.

It's often the case that, towards the end, we become elegiac – I think that is a real danger. I've spent my life and my career looking forward; I don't want to change the habit now. Besides which, the job of journalism isn't finished. It never will be. The pursuit of truth doesn't reach an end point. The truth is in a constant state of becoming.

Likewise, the battle for a more equal society is nowhere near concluded and, I suspect, never will be. Different societies at different times will have a different understanding of what constitutes equality of opportunity. It's right that they should – a democratic society is, at root, a society that has the freedom to disagree. Nevertheless, we need not be overly philosophical to see that we are heading for dark waters if we don't make urgent changes to our society. The inequality that has riven Britain must be addressed. We must, all of us, keep pushing the issue up the agenda, keep challenging the power of elites and keep fighting for equality.

I feel I still have a role to play in this, and I hope this book is some small part of that. In order to continue holding prime ministers, their Cabinets and the wider political elite to account, I don't think it's sensible for journalists to get too comfortable with the establishment. That's why I decided to turn down an OBE. If I am to meet and report on Johnson's successor, it is essential for me to maintain the same safe distance that I had with all his predecessors. I saw a joke once in the satirical magazine *Private Eye* that the OBE is the order of the brown nose. It's a fair claim, particularly fair if you're a journalist. It's quite a compromise to take an honour from the civic power that you're paid to report on, and, where relevant, criticize. A journalist, as far as possible, should not be beholden to anybody. If someone somewhat nearer to the heart of authority in this country deems that you are, as it were, on their side, I'm not sure you're doing your job properly.

And who is that person? Who is the appointer? No explanation comes. I felt suspicious of the honours system when I received word that somebody had seen fit to anoint me. There was no mention of my charity work, or my broadcasting. Just a message: Her Majesty the Queen sees fit to appoint Jon Snow as an Officer of the Order of the British Empire. Was it literally the Queen who made the decision? Was there a panel? Who is on it? How did they reach consensus?

Besides that, the titling tells us there is something amiss with our system. To be appointed to the Order of the British Empire, when the empire is dead as a duck, feels such a hollow way to be recognized. The empire may be dead, but I'm not. I may be a touch long in the tooth, but, as far as I'm aware, I haven't joined the ranks of the deceased. Beyond the empire's non-existence, there is the small matter of what it did when it was alive and kicking. Yes, there are certain things which have flowed from the empire that have fostered greater co-operation with others, such as the Commonwealth. But a lot of what was done in the name of empire – slavery being the most egregious example – are not things I wish to be associated with. OBE, CBE, KBE – Officer, Commander, Knight of the Order of the British Empire – it's a funny way to honour somebody to say, 'Congratulations, you've done such a good job that you can call yourself an esteemed soldier of a long-dead empire that used to go around the world enslaving people.' The honours system is evidence, were it needed, that the elite is in rude health in Britain.

I am mentioning this because it tends to be towards the end of somebody's career that they are offered such a reward. And I hope you can see that my refusal means that I'm not finished with journalism, nor with battling inequality. It was an intensely personal decision, but I did not wish to join the club. As an objective journalist I *couldn't* join the club. We journalists owe it to our consumers not to be beholden to any authority. We're paid to go out, look, come back and tell the story. How can you do that if you've been patted on the head by the establishment?

I hope, therefore, you can see that this decision was not idealistic but was, rather, of a piece with my career so far. My objective has always been to be a dependable source of information. A source that people can trust. Without sounding pompous, that's an important thing for society to have. People must make up their own minds in a democracy. There are events that happen in our lives every day of the week, every minute of every day. And people turn to journalists for an account of what's going on.

If they know that journalists are signed up to one element of the system, how are they going to trust them?

The state of us

This is not the time, therefore, for me to pull a chair up to the fireplace and start rattling on about the good old days. But it does provide me with an opportunity to reflect on the past – indeed, on my past – so that we might find some evidence of the most effective ways to strive for a better future. I hope, in this concluding chapter, to think through some of the changes I've seen in my lifetime, to journalism and to Britain more generally, and to think about what they tell us about inequality and how best we might tackle it. I want to close the case on why I feel equality matters, and even make some suggestions as to what we might do about it.

To do so, I will draw on three things that have been key to my own life and that have emerged time and time again throughout this book. I think they are pretty good rules of thumb that we can apply to collective life, too. They are *optimism* – the belief that things can, and do, get better; *meaningfulness* – the belief that what you do matters; and *community* – the belief that, despite our superficial differences, other people are by and large good and it's rewarding to live amongst them.

These three things provide a sort of key to how I've pursued my career. I am an optimist, who has tried to do his job without compromise, and who enjoys the company of others. I think they also provide a key to how we might go about continuing to build a society that we can be proud of.

I loved working on film because it gave you time to breathe. It had to be developed, and whilst it did there was a chance for you to sit down and think, 'What did I just witness?' You couldn't see what you had filmed because it was still being processed in chemicals. But you had enough notes, and enough sense of what you'd just seen, to begin to take a view. I miss the time and consideration that you had with film – it gave our reporting a certain stately measure. The two hours whilst technicians were developing it left me free to make phone calls, consult others, and if nothing else, sit down and simply think.

And yet video, and then digital, have been godsends. For journalists, they are wonderful inventions. Far more deployable and usable than film, they have been a bonus for my trade. Film may have given you breathing space whilst it was being developed, but it's incredible to think that during editing the editor would literally take the film, straighten it out from their pointed finger to their nose, and call it three seconds of footage. We were editing almost blind as we assembled our stories. New technologies have enabled us to be much more honest with the viewer. You've got something to play to yourself immediately as you're formulating your report. You can think to yourself, 'Is the story that I'm telling really represented in the footage we're showing?' and you can amend it, and your own analysis, before the broadcast.

This is how the future works. For me, new technology is a plus. But that's not to say we don't lose anything as we move forward. It is a case of both. You gain and you lose. And you gain. And you lose. The digital era has made that even more acute.

It may be that, in our digital age, we all lack that pause whilst the film develops. When we approach the news, there is less time to reflect – and the news itself is more knee-jerk than it was when your only access to it was via the morning paper or the evening broadcast. There's a danger that we are moving so quickly that we miss things. But that does not need to be the case. To return to my own example, back in the film era, News at Ten was completely dead by seven o'clock at night because anything you discovered after that wouldn't get on. I would never want to go back to the film age, and I feel I'm a much better journalist for having worked in the present age than if I'd retired having never known anything other than celluloid.

Whilst, obviously, it must be verified, we can now get incredible testimony from the phones that are in everybody's pockets. They are stitched very effectively into TV news broadcasts every day. This has been a boon in establishing the truth. Where there is an insurrection, a shooting or a dodgy deal being struck, journalists today have a source that they never had in the past. Now everyone has a camera in their pocket. For a television journalist, it has been a revolution.

It could well, in the future, act as a democratizing force too. One such moment that sticks out in my mind is the fallout following the murder of George Floyd in the United States. There had been multiple instances of police violence in the preceding years, but this murder was filmed on somebody's mobile phone and viewed across the world. It led to an enormous surge of support for a contemporary civil rights movement. Many of us have not yet woken fully to the power of the mobile phone; the individual has a vast amount of power right there in their pocket. Yes, there are drawbacks to this, as there are to all new technologies. But if you are an optimist you can see the potential of this technology, and you can draw on those upsides to achieve whatever your objective might be – just like when we changed from film to digital in the newsroom.

Optimism allows us to be open-minded and fluid. We often hear that technology is making things worse – that it has left us polarized, distracted and confused. Maybe it has. But it has done a great deal of other things, too. We could dwell on the fact that we no longer have thinking time whilst the film develops, or we could dwell on the fact that we can continue editing and updating the story in the minutes before it is broadcast – as an optimist, I choose the latter.

And, as an optimist, I think that the best news, by which I mean the best news production, is yet to come. There will be ever more technological changes, and the average journalist will have ever greater heaps of information to trawl through. But the potential is there for the news to become more accurate, and by extension more trust-worthy, than at any time before. Making the news more accurate and more trustworthy is part of my belief that meaningful work, work that makes a difference, is pos-sible and accessible to all of us. I believe that what you do matters, and I have been lucky to experience a couple of moments in my life when my own work has, in a small but observable way, made a difference in real time.

At an early stage of my career, I worked in Central America. At the time, it was relatively obscure to the British public: a liminal space at the bottom of the United States that nobody knew much about. My team and I did work there that I still think was special; I remain very proud of it. El Salvador, Nicaragua, Guatemala, Panama – we worked in all those places, and we produced, in my view, some excellent journalism. The work we did in El Salvador particularly stands out. It was an extraordinarily violent place. There was terrible repression by an extreme administration, a dictatorship in effect. The army was used liberally against its own people. I saw for the first time liberation theology in action – the Catholic Church militating against fascism. When I arrived, there was a full-scale rebellion by the people met by full-scale repression by the military authorities. It was a remarkable thing to witness.

There were very few other British journalists reporting. It was not a former British colony; Britain had no clear link with the place. There was no real reason why anyone back home should be particularly interested. Yet, for me, it was a watershed. As the story developed, it became fascinating, and terribly important, because it spoke directly to inequality, and to the way in which we are all connected. The people with the weapons were the people in charge, they amassed power and money; the people without were forced to suffer.

At the time, I was too busy reporting what I saw to sum it up in that way. Still, it was quite obvious to me when you saw bodies in the road, when you saw soldiers rounding up civilians, when you heard the sound of gunshots, that we were dealing with a lawless dictatorship. I also realized how complicated the world could be. The soldiers were drawn from the same pool as the people they were killing. They were being ordered to kill them by the dictatorship and were, in a strange way, both perpetrators and victims. Furthermore, the dictatorship sometimes operated with America's blessing; it was acting out its violence knowing it had the tacit support of the richest and most powerful country in the world. It wasn't a simple story. It never is when you look closely. But nevertheless, there were the ingredients there that I wanted to show to the world. They are the same ingredients that I've put into this book.

As I said, people at home in Britain were not aware of the problems in Central America. In reporting from there I had the good fortune to shine a light on an injustice. Whilst doing so did not fix the problem, nowhere near, a lot of problems that seemed completely intractable at that time are today in the process of being resolved. Salvadoreans are not killing each other on the same scale, though many of the divisions are still there. Those divisions will remain for years to come, but there are people trying to overcome them. El Salvador has taken a step in the right direction.

In part, shining a light on this massive inequality helped bring about that step in the right direction. At least I hope it did. It may only have been in a small and indirect way, but I think our reporting helped the English-speaking world begin to understand Central America. This had the effect, in the fullness of time, of causing the Americans to understand it. And, as mentioned, Uncle Sam was frustrating efforts to resolve matters. Journalism exposed what was being done under American auspices. It wasn't my job to decide who was right and who was wrong – merely to report what I saw, and thereby enable others to make up their own minds. With time, they did.

Collectively, we were part of the great project of bringing information to light and presenting it in a most vivid form. Mainstream television news reaches ordinary people, and it was ordinary people in Britain and America who pressured their governments to do something about the situation. That is to say, it mattered. It had an outcome. It wasn't just a kind of parlour game or an academic debate – the news-gathering system proved itself to be important. When I think about working for ITN, moments like that were always my joy.

I started life as an international correspondent, travelling around the world looking for stories. But in the last few years, it's issues here in Britain that have really stood out to me. The thread linking the stories I've been most drawn to over the course of my career – whether it's Amin's Uganda, Central America, Iran, Iraq, Brexit, Grenfell – is inequality. It has taken me most of my career to come to understand that, and it is worth me asking why. I think the reason is the third rule of thumb I mentioned above: community.

I came from the posh side of the railway tracks. I was shocked, really shocked, to encounter inequality as a young man – that's how naïve I was. Fortunately, I had just enough brain to spot the problem, and spot that it was poisonous and intolerable. Inequalities are corrosive. They wither our society. There is nothing good to be said about them. Everybody should be given a chance in life. And when we are thinking about everybody, we are thinking, ultimately about community. Fostering a community is not a purely natural and organic process. It requires effort, from individuals and from the state. That's, in fact, what a community is – different people pulling together to achieve a common object.

Giving people a chance is the most important thing. We must work together to create the conditions in which people obtain equality of opportunity. In raising the whole question of inequality, one can immediately be accused of being a lefty, or some sort of minor revolutionary. But I think we can all agree, in my case at least, that this simply can't be the case. If it was, for one thing ITN wouldn't have employed me. But besides that, I am not calling for the abolition of capitalism or the absolute redistribution of wealth – I am merely suggesting we should do more to foster communities.

I have tended to travel with the underdog. What has always struck me, though, is that the underdog usually has the comfort of being the majority. That's certainly true in Britain today. The majority of people are not given the opportunities that they might be. Seeing inequality in the raw, poverty in the flesh – the homeless person on the street, the food bank user, the recently arrived refugee, a victim of the violent whims of autocracy – makes me, and I believe most people, feel extremely uneasy. Inequality doesn't seem to any of us to be a natural inevitability of human existence and we have the means to ensure that it is not the case.

The first step is understanding. We need to recognize that there is a problem. Only then can we begin figuring out what resources we might marshal to overcome it. You can't understand anything unless you're told about it, and that has been my role; I did so because I thought that if people were aware of it, it was likely that they would feel the same way as I did. An example of this is South Africa. It's quite clear that apartheid – that enforced inequality through a dogma driven by the government of the day – did not produce a harmonious, opportunity-for-all kind of country. If you deliberately break a population down into the haves and the have nots, you will have a very unhappy place. So it proved.

When I first became involved, in my very minor way, in anti-apartheid activities, the attempt to dismantle apartheid seemed almost impossible. And yet, after years of struggle, apartheid is over and South Africa is now, if not a utopia, then at least a country without apartheid. It's progressing. My trigger to getting involved, as I have written elsewhere, was the realization that some of the children I was teaching in Uganda were much brighter, had a much greater level of what you might call raw intelligence, than me. But their lives were probably not likely to take the same trajectory as my own because they lacked the opportunities that I had. That struck me as wrong, and it powered me through the next five decades of life. The flicker of a sense of injustice that I took back to England was fanned into a flame by hearing more about the issues. By journalism.

When I look at young people today, the new wave of journalists I admire or activists I talk to, and I put my eighteen-year-old self in their shoes, the thing I most want to tell them is that the problems they see are not intractable. If they think that, they're wrong. Positive change can and does happen. Don't imagine that you become a better journalist, or anything else for that matter, by forsaking the things you believe in. I have always tested my beliefs. I always made them withstand contact with reality – I certainly never reported anything that I couldn't film but, equally, I always did what I believed in. I always tried to be true to my values. What can you do in your life if you haven't developed some values and tried to stay consistent to them? Very little, I'd wager. So, if ever people feel as though a better world isn't possible, I point them to the evidence of the present. I have been walking this beat for decades, and in that time have seen real, lasting and positive change. The world of yesterday I remember well. It would shock and appal these new journalists and activists whose work I admire. Trust me when I say that our present is better than our past, and if my life experiences are anything to go by, this will continue to be the case in the future.

Be brave

What, then, is the state of us?

Things are always better and worse than we think. Better, in that we rarely appreciate how much things have improved. Worse, in that we too often bury our head in the sand regarding how much better things could be. The message of this book, then, is not to simply point out inequalities. It is to do so in the hope that we will continue to put our collective shoulder against the wheel, in whatever way we are best able, so that we might drive them out of our lives.

When I look to the future, I look first and foremost at the heart of all our communities: the school. Hope for the future inevitably lies with our children, and most of the solutions to the problems that I've been talking about will be found in tomorrow's classroom. We in Britain must improve our attitudes to seemingly intransigent inequalities like race, class and gender. And the best place to start is in our schools. It's happening. We're beginning to grow closer to one another; we are beginning to reflect who we really are. Where and when that happens, it has a profound impact on living together, working together and coming together.

Irrespective of whether private education is a good thing or a bad thing, it is in the state-school sector that these opportunities most abundantly exist. The natural mixing of ethnicities, genders, classes is key to addressing equality of opportunity. Trying to do it later in life is harder. We aren't ever fixed, but I fear that we are more likely to become set in our ways as we age. Before I went to Uganda, I had all sorts of biases and prejudices. Thankfully, the experience changed me. Still, my cohort at the public school I attended was shaped in certain ways by the fact that we did not meet any Black people, or even any women, before we became, practically speaking, adults. That has had a deleterious effect on the lives of the people involved, and on the health of our society. We could have been so much more had we had the opportunity to embrace the reality of our society.

Power and wealth gravitate towards themselves, they pool and concentrate. But that is not our fate. It is a trend that can be, and has been, bucked. In my lifetime we have gone from Black people not being able to vote in certain US states to having a Black president, and now a Black female vice-president. One thinks of the United States as a pretty rough-and-tumble place when it comes to ethnicity. But actually, inequality is being eroded even there. People claim that Kamala Harris or Barack Obama are exceptions that prove the rule. Not a bit of it. I think it's a very exciting time. We're seeing movement. There is change afoot.

On these matters, Britain has moved rather slowly. Yet we have clearly been enriched by the influx of ethnic minorities, by women taking up their rightful place in the workforce, and in the less privileged attending universities. We are a society with massive potential as a result. If we can utilize it properly, Britain's diversity gives it an advantage over many of its competitor countries, and we can expect great things in its near future. Yes, there can be teething problems, and there have been, but there's no doubt we're moving forward on these issues. The conversation is in a completely different place to where it was even a decade ago, let alone five.

I am a real optimist when it comes to race, class and gender. It's my belief that eventually there will come a true democracy – a society in which all the people, all the time, are represented. In which Britain is owned and run by its people. One area where this is discernible is the welfare state. I believe in the welfare state. It is the political manifestation of community. I feel Britain still is a welfare state, like it or not. Welfarism is now embedded in British culture, and I don't think any government will get very far by trying to demolish it. There are too many elements that are cherished by the British people, not least our health service. There has never been a more testing time for a health service than the recent pandemic and we're still coming through it. But we have weathered this terrible storm because we have a world-class health service, and people know it. The British electorate will never consciously let it go. The job of journalists is to make sure that people are conscious of any attempt to dismantle it.

As a reporter, I would make it a priority to watch what happens to our welfare state very carefully. Journalism may have taken its eye off this particular ball because there are so many others to look at. At the moment, the welfare state is not faring at its very best. As I write, we've been through a phase of cuts; these were deep, but I think the government has recently discovered that it couldn't effectively do away with the welfare state without paying in some other area. The government, and I suspect subsequent governments regardless of party, will be forced to consolidate where it's good and save where it's wasteful, which is as it should be: the welfare state shouldn't be inefficient. It must serve a purpose. Still, I don't think anybody will win votes in the years after the pandemic by saying, 'Sick pay, what an extravagance!' So improve the welfare state, yes. Make it more rational, more integrated, of course. But lose it? Absolutely not. It is the living, breathing manifestation of the promise we make to each other as a community.

And community is everything, it is the essence of the good life. If you haven't had experience of it, now is the time to go and embrace it. In the end, to borrow from John Donne, no person is an island. We all have a contribution to make. We secretly know it, but often fool ourselves into believing we might not be capable of it. If you put down this book and take just one thought away from it, make it this: be brave. The reward for being so is mighty. When you work with and for others, when you engage in the world with optimism, you do something hugely meaningful. You grow into something so much greater than yourself. You grow into 'us'.

ACKNOWLEDGEMENTS

With thanks to Jonny Geller, Alex Christofi, Jack Ramm, Sharika Teelwah and Gilly Nolan in helping to bring this book into the light of day.

NOTES

CHAPTER 1: WAKE-UP CALL

1 https://www.bbc.co.uk/news/stories-42072477

2 https://blogs.lse.ac.uk/pulsedv/lse-visualising-data-inequality-in-the-uk/

3 Ibid.

4 https://www.statista.com/statistics/382695/uk-foodbank-users/

5 https://onlinelibrary.wiley.com/doi/full/10.1111/1467-923X.12621 This isn't simply my intuition, inequality within the housing market 'strongly predicted the vote for Leave or Remain': 'Over the last three decades, the British housing market has undergone a rapid transformation. In the post-war era, British housing featured high levels of social housing and low levels of housing wealth inequality. Today – following a mass social housing sell-off and a historic boom in asset prices – it features the inverse. We argue that this transformation has had a profound impact on British politics by dividing regions, tenures, and generations in a new housing cleavage.
To make this case, we examine the recent history of British housing and its relationship to political changes both past and future. We begin by arguing that the performance of the British housing market – both the cause and the effect of local economic fortunes – shaped attitudes toward Britain's relationship to the European Union by structuring voters' sense of inclusion in the project of international integration. We argue that house prices, even *at a highly disaggregated local level, strongly predicted the vote for Leave or Remain.*'

6   https://ifs.org.uk/publications/14827
7   https://equalitytrust.org.uk/how-has-inequality-changed
8   https://archives.history.ac.uk/history-in-focus/welfare/articles/glennersterh.html#:~:text=In%201937%20social%20policy%20reduced,as%20much%20as%20in%201937
9   https://www.kingsfund.org.uk/publications/whats-happening-life-expectancy-england
10 https://www.youtube.com/watch?v=xqD7P1RgzcQ

CHAPTER 2: THE OLD WAYS

1   https://www.theguardian.com/politics/2006/aug/27/uk.conservatives1
2   https://www.parliament.uk/globalassets/documents/commons-information-office/g07.pdf
3   https://researchbriefings.files.parliament.uk/documents/SN07104/SN07104.pdf
4   https://commonslibrary.parliament.uk/research-briefings/cbp-7483/
5   It was he who established the eponymous 'Salisbury Convention', a compromise whereby the House of Lords cannot refuse to pass Bills more than three times if the government had them in their manifesto to the electorate.

CHAPTER 3: WHERE WE LIVE

1   https://data.justice.gov.uk/prisons
2   https://www.cdbb.cam.ac.uk/system/files/documents/3.PositionPaperGovernanceMaintenanceandFacilitiesManagement_web.pdf
3   https://www.emerald.com/insight/content/doi/10.1108/IJSE-04-2017-0167/full/html

4   https://www.ojp.gov/ncjrs/virtual-library/abstracts/
     does-poverty-cause-domestic-violence-some-answer-lima

CHAPTER 4: BREXIT AND BACKLASH

1   https://www.reuters.com/article/
     us-britain-thatcher-quotes-idUKBRE9370LI20130408
2   https://www.theguardian.com/politics/2013/jun/28/
     boris-johnson-popular-capable-pm-poll
3   https://www.theguardian.com/politics/2016/oct/16/secret-
     boris-johnson-column-favoured-uk-remaining-in-eu
4   Ibid.
5   https://www.ipsos.com/en-uk/economistipsos-mori-
     december-2015-issues-index
6   https://www.ipsos.com/en-uk/issues-index-april-2019-public-
     concern-over-brexit-reaches-record-high
7   https://commonslibrary.parliament.uk/
     brexit-the-people-vs-parliament/
8   https://www.theguardian.com/business/2016/mar/15/
     cbi-member-survey-reveals-huge-support-for-remaining-
     in-eu
9   https://www.theguardian.com/politics/2016/jun/05/
     trade-union-members-should-vote-to-stay-in-the-eu
10 https://www.newstatesman.com/politics/2016/10/
     arron-banks-the-man-who-bought-brexit
11 https://www.youtube.com/watch?v=lgoEuHjplfI
12 Ibid.

CHAPTER 5: ASYMMETRIC WAR, UNEQUAL
PEACE

1   https://yougov.co.uk/topics/politics/articles-reports/2015/
     06/03/remembering-iraq

2   https://www.macrotrends.net/countries/GBR/united-
    kingdom/military-spending-defense-budget
3   https://www.washingtonpost.com/politics/2022/02/25/words-
    deeds-putin-shows-hes-rejecting-even-soviet-era-borders/
4   https://borgenproject.org/income-inequality-in-russia/
5   https://fortune.com/2022/03/02/vladimir-putin-net-worth-2022/

CHAPTER 7: PRESS FREEDOM

1   https://www.theguardian.com/uk-news/2014/jan/31/footage-
    released-guardian-editors-snowden-hard-drives-gchq

CHAPTER 8: THE NEXT GENERATION

1   https://assets.publishing.service.gov.uk/government/uploads/
    system/uploads/attachment_data/file/811045/Elitist_Britain_
    2019.pdf
2   Ibid
3   Ibid.
4   https://static1.squarespace.com/
    static/58ed40453a04116f46e8d99b/t/5d275769b2a56d00017de
    b2f/1562859421693/Job+Creators
5   https://www.theguardian.com/world/2020/jun/20/
    clive-myrie-details-racist-abuse-he-receives-as-bbc-news-
    presenter
6   https://blog.policy.manchester.ac.uk/featured/2014/08/
    the-decline-of-racial-prejudice-in-britain/

INDEX

ABOUT THE AUTHOR

One of the nation's pre-eminent broadcasters, **Jon Snow** was the face of Channel 4 News from 1989 to 2021. In that time, he has reported in dozens of countries, from the fall of the Berlin Wall to Barack Obama's inauguration, interviewing countless world leaders and cultural icons. His many awards include a BAFTA fellowship, the Richard Dimbleby BAFTA award for Best Factual Contribution to Television (2005), and Royal Television Society awards for Journalist of the Year (2005 and 2006) and Presenter of the Year (2009, 2010 and 2012). He collected the BAFTA award for news coverage for the 2011 Channel 4 News coverage of the Japanese tsunami and delivered the prestigious MacTaggart Lecture at Edinburgh's International Television Festival in 2017. He is the author of two books: *Shooting History* and *The State of Us*.